The Winter Soldier Investigation

The
Winter Soldier
Investigation

An Inquiry into
American War Crimes

By the Vietnam Veterans
Against the War

Beacon Press

Copyright © 1972 by the Vietnam Veterans Against the War, Inc.
Library of Congress catalog card number: 74-179157
International Standard Book Number: 0-8070-0250-X (hardcover)
0-8070-0251-8 (paperback)
Beacon Press books are published under the auspices
of the Unitarian Universalist Association
Published simultaneously in Canada by Saunders of Toronto, Ltd.
All rights reserved
Printed in the United States of America

This book is dedicated to you,

America

Now,
Before the napalm-scorched earth
consumes the blood
of
would-be-fathers
and
have-been-sons
of
daughters spread-eagled
and
mothers on the run.
Reflect.
See what you've become,

Amerika.

A. H.

These are the times that try men's souls. The summer soldier and the sunshine patriot will in this crisis shrink from the service of his country; but he that stands it now, deserves the love and thanks of man and woman.

—*Tom Paine*

CONTENTS

PREFACE

Most "war crimes" are committed by people who feel they have some kind of permission for what they do—even to the point of feeling righteous—and who commonly regard their victims as less than human. Dehumanization provides the means of tolerating mass destruction or genocide. The psychic restrictions against the taking of human life that have become a part of civilized man, cannot be called into play when those who are to be destroyed have been divested of their humanness.

The Winter Soldier Investigation was convened in Detroit, Michigan, on January 31 and February 1, 2, 1971, because veterans of the Indochina war knew that the occurrence at My Lai was not an isolated incident, and many felt they could not allow the people of this country to be deceived by such statements as "They must have gone berserk" and "My Lai was clearly an aberration on the part of a junior officer and the small group of men he commanded."

My Lai was only a minor step beyond the standard, official United States in Indochina. It is hypocritical self-righteousness to condemn the soldiers at My Lai without condemning those who set the criminal policy of free-fire zones, strategic hamlets, saturation bombing, etcetera, from which My Lai was the inevitable result.

Furthermore, we felt that it was absolutely imperative to let the American people know how the motivation to carry out the criminal policy is developed through dehumanization, and how atrocities that go beyond the pale of official policy (though they certainly are in the realm of *de facto* policy) are perpetrated with such indifference.

During the three days of hearings more than one hundred veterans and sixteen civilians gave firsthand testimony to war crimes which they either committed or witnessed. They testified in panels arranged by combat units and, where possible, in chronological order from the time of the first acknowledged U.S. troops in Vietnam to clearly show the consistency in the development and implementation of the criminal policy through the succession of administrations and top military commanders. Besides the combat units, there were panels on weaponry, medical care, prisoners of war, racism, the devastation of Vietnam, and the psychological effects of the war on the American soldiers.

The verbatim transcript of the investigation runs to almost a thousand pages. In this abridged edition, the panel structure has been abandoned to allow the testimony of some seventy-five veterans, as well as the statements from four civilians, to reflect the agonized experience shared by hundreds of thousands of Americans and Indochinese.

During the three days of hearings no phony indictments were handed down, no verdict reached, and no attempt made to create an illusion of judiciary proceedings. The purpose of the hearings was not to punish but to preclude the continuance of man's inhumanity to his fellow man.

The crimes against humanity, the war itself, might not have occurred if we, all of us, had not been brought up in a country permeated with racism, obsessed with communism, and convinced beyond a shadow of doubt that we are good and most other countries are inherently evil.

Crimes are committed by people. "Reflect, see what WE'VE become, Amerika."

Al Hubbard
Executive Secretary
Vietnam Veterans Against the War

September 15, 1971

ACKNOWLEDGMENTS

The Winter Soldier Investigation was the result of many months of sometimes tedious, often difficult, always emotionally draining work on the part of a great many people, inside and outside of VVAW.

We are especially grateful to Madelyn Moore, Nina Kimche, Jane Fonda, Winterfilm, Inc., Mark Lane, Carol Agusta, Caroline Muggar, Joel Flesch, Chris Stratef, Dick Gregory, Phil Ochs, Graham Nash, Dave Crosby, Bruce Engell, Alison Montgomery, Rick Millen, Verna Marone, Lucille More, Dorothy Hage, Peggy McEneaney, Sam Sade, Polly Walker, Tomar Levine, Eileen Carey, Barbara Dane, Donald Sutherland, Steve Jaffe, Caroline Weeks; and we also gratefully acknowledge the dedication and sacrifice of all the veterans who participated in the Winter Soldier Investigation.

OPENING STATEMENT

Lt. William Crandell, Americal Division

"Over the border they send us to kill and to fight for a cause they've long ago forgotten." These lines of Paul Simon's recall to the Vietnam Veterans the causes for which we went to fight in Vietnam and the outrages we were part of because the men who sent us had long ago forgotten the meaning of the words.

We went to preserve the peace and our testimony will show that we have set all of Indochina aflame. We went to defend the Vietnamese people and our testimony will show that we are committing genocide against them. We went to fight for freedom and our testimony will show that we have turned Vietnam into a series of concentration camps.

We went to guarantee the right of self-determination to the people of South Vietnam and our testimony will show that we are forcing a corrupt and dictatorial government upon them. We went to work toward the brotherhood of man and our testimony will show that our strategy and tactics are permeated with racism. We went to protect America and our testimony will show why our country is being torn apart by what we are doing in Vietnam.

In the bleak winter of 1776, when the men who had enlisted in the summer were going home because the way was hard and their enlistments were over, Tom Paine wrote, "These are the times that try men's souls. The summer soldier and the sunshine patriot will in this crisis shrink from the service of his country; but he that stands it now deserves the love and thanks of man and woman." Like the winter soldiers of 1776 who stayed after they had served their time, we veterans of Vietnam know that America is in grave danger. What threatens our country is not Redcoats or even Reds; it is our crimes that are destroying our national unity by separating those of our countrymen who deplore these acts from those

1

of our countrymen who refuse to examine what is being done in America's name.

The Winter Soldier Investigation is not a mock trial. There will be no phony indictments; there will be no verdict against Uncle Sam. Over a hundred Vietnam veterans will present straightforward testimony—direct testimony—about acts which are war crimes under international law. Acts which these men have seen and participated in. Acts which are the inexorable result of national policy.

It has often been remarked but seldom remembered that war itself is a crime. Yet a war crime is more and other than war. It is an atrocity beyond the usual barbaric bounds of war. It is legal definition growing out of custom and tradition supported by every civilized nation in the world, including our own. It is an act beyond the pale of acceptable actions even in war. Deliberate killing or torturing of prisoners of war is a war crime. Deliberate destruction without military purpose of civilian communities is a war crime. The use of certain arms and armaments and of gas is a war crime. The forcible relocation of population for any purpose is a war crime. All of these crimes have been committed by the U. S. Government over the past ten years in Indochina. An estimated one million South Vietnamese civilians have been killed because of these war crimes. A good portion of the reported 700,000 National Liberation Front and North Vietnamese soldiers killed have died as a result of these war crimes and no one knows how many North Vietnamese civilians, Cambodian civilians, and Laotian civilians have died as a result of these war crimes.

But we intend to tell more. We intend to tell who it was that gave us those orders; that created that policy; that set that standard of war bordering on full and final genocide. We intend to demonstrate that My Lai was no unusual occurrence, other than, perhaps, the number of victims killed all in one place, all at one time, all by one platoon of us. We intend to show that the policies of Americal Division which inevitably resulted in My Lai were the policies of other Army and Marine divisions as well. We intend to show that the war crimes in Vietnam did not start in March 1968, or in the village of Son My or with one Lieutenant William Calley. We intend to indict those really responsible for My Lai, for Vietnam, for attempted genocide. General Westmoreland said in 1966, "I'd like to say that let one fact be clear. As far as the U. S. Military Assistance Command in Vietnam is concerned, one mishap, one innocent civilian killed, one civilian wounded, or one dwelling needlessly destroyed is too many. By its very nature war is destructive, and historically civilians have suffered. But the war in Vietnam is different; it is designed by the insurgents and the aggressors to be fought among the people many of whom are not participants in or closely identified with the struggle. People, more than terrain, are the objectives in this war and we will not and cannot be callous about those people. We are sensitive to these incidents and want no more of them. If one does occur, mistake or accident, we intend to search it carefully for any lesson that will help us improve our procedures and our controls. We realize we have a great problem and I can assure you we are attacking it aggressively."

We need not judge Westmoreland's bland assurances nor need we pass responsibility for these crimes. You who hear or read our testimony will be able to conclude for yourselves who is responsible. We are here to bear witness not against America, but against those policymakers who are perverting America. We echo Mark Twain's indictment of the war crimes committed during the Philippine insurrection: "We have invited our clean young men to shoulder a discredited musket and do bandit's work under a flag which bandits have been accustomed to fear, not to follow."

We cannot conceal from ourselves that privately we are a little troubled about our uniform. It is one of our prides; it is acquainted with honor; it is familiar with great deeds and noble. We love it; we revere it. And so this errand it is on makes us uneasy. And our flag, another pride of ours, the chiefest. We have worshiped it so and when we have seen it in far lands, glimpsing it unexpectedly in that strange sky, waving its welcome and benediction to us, we have caught our breaths and uncovered our heads for a moment for the thought of what it was to us and the great ideals it stood for.

3

Indeed, we must do something about these things. It is easily managed. We can have just our usual flag with the white stripes painted black and the stars replaced by the skull and crossbones.

We are ready to let the testimony say it all.

II. "YOU'VE GOTTA GO TO VIETNAM, YOU'VE GOTTA KILL THE GOOKS."

Cpl. John Geymann, 3rd Marine Division

Well, Marine training starts from the first day you get into boot camp and doesn't end till the day you're discharged. When you're told something to do, whether to go to the bathroom or have a cigarette, or whether you go to bed or you get some free time to write a letter, you preface it or you end it with VC, or gook or slope, kill-kill-kill. That's all you're told to do. Everything is done on a threat basis; if you don't do things the way you're supposed to do, this is what's going to happen to you. If you go to Vietnam, and you don't kill the gooks, this is what's going to happen to you. If you don't defend freedom in Vietnam, the gooks are going to be here. They're going to be in California, they're going to be in Detroit, they're going to be in Windsor, they're going to be all over you. You've gotta go to Vietnam, you've gotta kill the gooks. They're no good. In Com School I was in the hospital. Even in the hospitals, they're passing out pictures of mutilated bodies, showing this is what we do to the gooks, this is what's fun to do with the gooks. When somebody asks, "Why do you do it to a gook, why do you do this to people?" your answer is, "So what, they're just gooks, they're not people. It doesn't make any difference what you do to them; they're not human." And this thing is built into you, it's thrust into your head from the moment you wake up in boot camp to the moment you wake up when you're a civilian. And it's a very hard thing to try and forget about it. It's about the only way I can put it, it's—they make you want to kill. Their whole thing is killing. You're not to question, you're not to ask why. If you're told to kill, you're to kill. You're not supposed to say why or who says so? Or why should I kill this person? For what reason? How is it benefiting me? How are they hurting me? It's just to be a machine. When you're wound up and when your button is

5

pushed, you've gotta react. If you don't react the way they want you to, you're in trouble with them.

Sgt. Michael McCusker, 1st Marine Division

Now, within your own conscience, in the spectrum of war, that whole Vietnam thing is based on fear. You're scared to death all the way over there. You're told continually that you're going to die if you don't do this, if you don't do that. That every Vietnamese is going to kill you; that booby-trapped babies are going to be sent against you and old grand-mothers are going to throw bombs at you, which can be very, very true and in many instances *is* true; but the question is not asked why that old grandmother wants to throw a bomb at you. That's the part of the discussion that doesn't occur.

Sgt. Joe Bangert, 1st Marine Division

You can check with the Marines who have been to Viet-nam—your last day in the States at staging battalion at Camp Pendleton you have a little lesson and it's called the rabbit lesson, where the staff NCO comes out and he has a rabbit and he's talking to you about escape and evasion and survival in the jungle. He has this rabbit and then in a couple of sec-onds after just about everyone falls in love with it—not falls in love with it, but, you know, they're humane there—he cracks it in the neck, skins it, disembowels it. He does this to the rabbit—and then they throw the guts out into the audi-ence. You can get anything out of that you want, but that's your last lesson you catch in the United States before you leave for Vietnam where they take that rabbit and they kill it, and they skin it, and they play with its organs as if it's trash and they throw the organs all over the place and then these guys are put on the plane the next day and sent to Vietnam.

6

III. "AND ALL OF THEM CAN BE KILLED AND MOST OF THEM ARE KILLED."

Pfc. Allen Akers, 3rd Marine Division

I am 25 years old and from the city of Chicago. I joined the Marines just after high school and was in Echo Company, 2nd Battalion, 4th Marines, Infantry Unit. I am presently in college and work for the YMCA. I was in Vietnam from May of '65 until March of '66.

We were given orders whenever we moved into a village to reconnoiter by fire. This means to—whenever we step into a village to fire upon houses, bushes, anything to our discretion that looked like there might be somebody hiding behind or in or under. What we did was we'd carry our rifles about hip high and we'd line up on line parallel to the village and start walking, firing from the hip. There were times when Vietnamese villages had man-made bomb shelters to protect themselves from air raids. Well, sometimes when we'd come to a village a Vietnamese would run out of the bomb shelter for fear of being caught, so consequently this surprise would startle any individual and they would automatically turn and fire, thereby uselessly killing civilians without giving them a chance.

Cpl. Jonathan Birch, 3rd Marine Division

I'm 24. I live in Philadelphia. I joined the Marine Corps right after high school. I was a corporal in B Company, 3rd Shore Party Battalion attached to 4th Marine Division. I landed in Chu Lai South Vietnam in 1965, in May. I was a field radio operator and presently I'm employed as an accountant in Philadelphia.

On the beach where we landed was a fishing village up in the northern edge of Dung Quai Bay. It was perhaps 5 to 10 huts. These people had been fishermen all their lives. They knew nothing but fishing, but since the Americans—the

7

military—wanted to use that area they moved them up a river, about a mile and a half up the coast. Now they were still fishermen and could still go out, but they were suspected of being VC. They weren't VC. They were just fishermen and you have to go out every day if you're going to earn your living by fishing. So they decided we'll move them up the river further still where we can keep a closer eye on them. They did that and then, just about August, they moved them into a relocation village which was off the river. They took their boats away, burned them, and gave them land and said, "All right, now you can become farmers. People need food and we don't trust fishermen." We personally took some of their little round boats—they look like little sampans—these little round things, called bull boats. So these people who had been fishermen for generations now suddenly became farmers on land that could not be farmed because the area in and around Chu Lai on the beach was sand; very dry, rotten sand.

Pfc. Charles Stephens, 101st Airborne Division

I served with the 1st Brigade, 3/27, 101st Airborne Division as a medic. I went over in 1965, in December 1965, and I stayed until February '67. When I first got to Phan Rang, our base camp, our battalion commander said we were going to leave Phan Rang—going to Tui Hoa. And we'd be in Tui Hoa anywhere from three weeks to three months. And I believe we were gone about a year and seven days. But before we left he told us, he said, "Don't worry. I know you guys are impatient, but when you get to Tui Hoa there'll be enough VC to go around." Also, the chaplain added that it's better to give than to receive and do unto others before they do unto you.

When we got to Tui Hoa the first battle we were in was in Happy Valley. And at Happy Valley we got quite a few of the people from our brigade killed. The very next operation I went on every village we went into we'd recon by fire, and in one village we wounded women and kids going into the village. When we got in there (this was in Tui Hoa), me and

8

another guy were treating two unconscious babies—not babies but like five- and six-year-old kids and a woman lying in a hammock. I told the lieutenant that these people had to be evacuated because if not evacuated (this lady and these kids had shrapnel and they were unconscious) I said they're gonna die. And he said, "Well, forget it, doc; we don't have time to stay and wait."

We went up on the hill right above this same village and we fired down on this village the next day while the people were trying to bury their dead, while they were doing their burial ceremony. And killed another person in the village. The people, they didn't wait to see if the guy was dead or not. They just rolled him over and put him in the hole with the others and covered him up. We went down that same day to get some water and there were two little boys playing on a dike and one sergeant just took his M-16 and shot one boy at the dike. The other boy tried to run. He was almost out of sight when this other guy, a Spec 4, shot this other little boy off the dike. The little boy was like lying on the ground kicking, so he shot him again to make sure he was dead.

Then we went into the village and this pappa-san, I don't know if he was a village chief or who he was, but he came up to us, he was telling us, he was making motions that a bird was flying over and the bird took a shit and a thing went boom-boom. He was saying this was how a lot of the people in the village got hurt. I told the lieutenant and the lieutenant still wouldn't have the people evacuated. So, every operation we went on after that, after our Happy Valley, they didn't believe our body counts. So we had to cut off the right ear of everybody we killed to prove our body count. I guess it was company SOP, or battalion SOP, but nothing was ever said to you. Guys would cut off heads, put them on a stake and stick a guy's penis in his mouth.

We had been on an ambush for about two weeks on the Ho Chi Minh Trail but we were supposed to be in Cambodia. The first week that we were there, we didn't fire at any of the enemy. We just watched them come down, and I guess further down the trail they were being knocked off. I don't know. But the second week we were told when anything

9

came down this trail, we were to shoot. About two-thirty one morning this lady and a little boy and a dog came walking down this trail (they did this every night) and the lady made some kind of funny sign with a lantern. This particular night a guy met her on a bicycle. She went back to her house alone, but this guy stayed on her trail and a few minutes later some more guys came and joined him. As they were coming down the trail, we knocked them off.

They said we were not supposed to use CS gas. We threw CS gas and the whole business.

SP/4 Kenneth Ruth, 1st Air Cavalry Division

I am a police officer and am currently working on a master's degree in education. My job while in the service was medic. I was attached out to different companies at different times. I'd just like to say that each of us could go on all day talking about atrocities that we witnessed, every veteran in here, not just the guys up here. Each of us saw many, and many of them we all participated in, so I am not going to run into a whole bunch that I saw. I'd just like to name a few.

At one time we were securing, which means that we set up a perimeter and you know you might sit there for four, five, six, seven days, and so we wanted to make sure our weapons were in order. What you do is you test-fire your weapons, just shoot 'em off for about two minutes or so into the distance. Well, many of us knew that on the other side of these bushes, out in front of us, was a whole village of people, and that if we did test-fire our weapons, those people would be in jeopardy. So I approached the platoon leader and the platoon sergeant and told them that there were civilians on the other side of the village beyond the bushes. I was told first of all by the platoon leader that he just didn't care, and when I told the platoon sergeant about it, he said he'd shoot a Montagnard as fast as he would a Cong, so it didn't make any difference to him. Nobody else cared. This is the general attitude. You know, Vietnamese aren't humans, they're targets. And one other thing I'd just like to point out

10

is when I was attached to the Special Forces, once in a while they needed a medic, I usually "volunteered" to go along with them.

I'd also like to point out some of the intelligence and modern interrogation methods used by the modern and sophisticated war machine. First of all we go into the village and ask people who they think are Viet Cong. So we were given two people that we were told were Viet Cong. What we do, is we took these two guys out in the field and we strung one of 'em up in a tree by his arms, tied his hands behind him, and then hung him in the tree. Now what we did to this man when we strung him up is that he was stripped of all his clothes, and then they tied a string around his testicles and a man backed up about ten feet and told him what would happen if he didn't answer any questions the way they saw fit. Now all we had to go by was that we were told that he was a suspect by other villagers. Now the other villagers weren't going to point out themselves, and somebody had to be pointed out.

So they'd ask a guy a question: "Do you know of any enemy units in this area?" and if he said, "No," the guy that was holding that string would just yank on it as hard as he could about ten times, and this guy would be just flying all over the place in pain. And this is what they used—I mean anybody's just going to say anything in a situation like this to get answers out of him. And then when they were done, when the guy was just limp and hanging there, the South Vietnamese indigenous troops, who worked with the Special Forces, went up there and then to get kicks, would run their knife through his ear and carve little superficial wounds on his body, not deep ones, but just you know, trickle it down his body to make fun of the guy. We took a guy to the other end of the village, and we didn't do this, all we did was burn his penis with a cigarette to get answers out of him. I'm sure people understand what that would be like if it was done to yourself or to your children.

This is just one of the things I saw. I could just go on all day. All of us could. And every GI in this room could say the same thing. But it's not just us. Everybody knows this. It

11

isn't just Lieutenant Calley. I was involved; I know there are so many other people involved in all this American policy in Vietnam.

Sgt. Scott Camil, 1st Marine Division

I was in the 1st Battalion, 11th Marines, attached to the 1st Battalion, 1st Marines, from March 1966 to November 1967. I was a forward observer in Vietnam. I went in right after high school and I'm a student now. My testimony involves burning of villages with civilians in them, the cutting off of ears, cutting off of heads, torturing of prisoners, calling in of artillery on villages for games, corpsmen killing wounded prisoners, napalm dropped on villages, women being raped, women and children being massacred, CS gas used on people, animals slaughtered, Chieu Hoi passes rejected and the people holding them shot, bodies shoved out of helicopters, tear-gassing people for fun and running civilian vehicles off the road.

About the calling in of artillery for games. The way it was worked would be the mortar forward observers would pick out certain houses in villages—friendly villages—and the mortar forward observers would call in mortars until they destroyed that house and then the artillery forward observer would call in artillery until he destroyed another house and whoever used the least amount of artillery, they won. And when we got back someone would have to buy someone else beers.

The cutting off of heads on Operation Stone: There was a lieutenant colonel there and two people had their heads cut off and put on stakes and stuck in the middle of the field. And we were notified that there was press covering the Operation and that we couldn't do that any more. Before we went out on the Operation we were told not to waste our heat tablets on food but to save them for the villages because we were going to destroy all the villages and we didn't give the people any time to get out of the villages. We just went in and burned them and if people were in the villages yelling

12

and screaming, we didn't help them. We just burned the houses as we went. We'd throw the heat tabs in because it was quicker and they'd keep burning. They couldn't put the heat tabs out. We'd throw them on top of the houses.

People cut off ears, and when they'd come back in off of an operation you'd make deals before you'd go out and like for every ear you cut off someone would buy you two beers, so people cut off ears. The torturing of prisoners was done with beatings and I saw one case where there were two prisoners. One prisoner was staked out on the ground and he was cut open while he was alive and part of his insides were cut out and they told the other prisoner if he didn't tell them what they wanted to know they would kill him. And I don't know what he said because he spoke in Vietnamese but then they killed him after that anyway.

Moderator: Were these primarily civilians or do you believe that they were, or do you know that they were actual NVA?

Camil: The way that we distinguished between civilians and VC, VC had weapons and civilians didn't and anybody that was dead was considered a VC. If you killed someone they said, "How do you know he's a VC?" and the general reply would be, "He's dead," and that was sufficient. When we went through the villages and searched people the women would have all their clothes taken off and the men would use their penises to probe them to make sure they didn't have anything hidden anywhere; and this was raping but it was done as searching.

Moderator: As searching. Were there officers present there?

Camil: Yes, there were.

Moderator: Was this on a company level?

Camil: Company level.

Moderator: The company commander was around when this happened?

Camil: Right.

Moderator: Did he approve of it or did he look the other way or?

Camil: He never said not to or never said anything about

13

it. The main thing was that if an operation was covered by the press there were certain things we weren't supposed to do, but if there was no press there, it was okay. I saw one case where a woman was shot by a sniper, one of our snipers. When we got up to her she was asking for water. And the lieutenant said to kill her. So he ripped off her clothes, they stabbed her in both breasts, they spread her eagle and shoved an E tool up her vagina, an entrenching tool, and she was still asking for water. And then they took that out and they used a tree limb and then she was shot.

Moderator: Did the men in your outfit or when you witnessed these things, did they seem to think that it was all right to do anything to the Vietnamese?

Camil: It wasn't like they were humans. We were conditioned to believe that this was for the good of the nation, the good of our country, and anything we did was okay. And when you shot someone you didn't think you were shooting at a human. They were a gook or a Commie and it was okay. And anything you did to them was okay because like they would tell you they'd do it to you if they had the chance.

Moderator: This was told you all through your training, then, in boot camp, in advanced training, and so forth and it was followed on then, right on through it?

Camil: Definitely.

Moderator: There's a program in Vietnam called the Chieu Hoi program where they leaflet and they pass out these passes where the enemy, the NVA, or the VC with these passes can get safe conduct and be treated as respected human beings not as POWs. But we have an instance—Mr. Camil, could you go into this?—where Chieu Hois were shot and their passes were rejected.

Camil: We understood what the Chieu Hois were for but we were told why should these people be able to shoot at us and then run and when they got close to being captured, come out with it and get away with it. So when they came out with it, we just shot them.

Moderator: Was this on orders or . . . ?

Camil: It was on orders.

14

Moderator: And what was done with the Chieu Hoi pass after the person was killed?

Camil: Any time a person was killed if they had any identification or passes or anything that would get us in trouble, they were destroyed.

Moderator: The platoon commander was present when this happened?

Camil: Definitely.

Moderator: Mr. Camil, you have testimony here of napalm being dropped on villagers. Could you go into this and kind of let us know what napalm is and how it was used and any of the results?

Camil: I really don't know that much about what it is or what it's made of. I just know that when it gets on you it burns and when they drop it from the planes, they usually drop two big cannisters of napalm at a time. It just burns everything up, including the people. Many times we've called in air before we'd go into a village, or if we had a village where we'd lost people because of booby traps, we'd call in napalm and it just burns down the village and the people.

Moderator: Wasn't it usually normal, or so-called operating procedure, you don't fire until fired on, and on these villages did you usually receive a lot of fire from them of the type that would say, we can't take the village, you'll have to call in napalm?

Camil: No, most of the time it was for safety. We'd napalm it first before we'd even go in just to make sure we wouldn't lose any men without any fire whatsoever. It was just for our protection, supposedly.

SP/4 Eugene Keys, 25th Infantry Division

I was in the 3rd Squadron, 4th Cavalry of the 25th Division. I'll be talking about forced relocation of civilians.

We were in an operation in Ho Bo Woods, I believe it was Cedar Falls or Junction City in January of 1967. We came across a village of women, young kids, and old men—no young men. We surrounded the village, then we forced all the

15

civilians out to an open field and we called in a Chinook, a large helicopter. At gunpoint we held these people until the Chinook arrived. Then we forced all of them onto the chopper to be taken to Saigon, I believe, and then we destroyed all of their hootches, we dumped all the rice down in their wells, killed all the fowl and the livestock, and left the place a real scorched earth.

L/Cpl. Paul Williams, 3rd Marine Division

I'm from Fayetteville, Arkansas. I served from May of 1966 to June of 1967 in the 1st and 3rd Marine Divisions. I was a Lance Corporal and I was a Forward Observer in the field.

Among other things that I witnessed were POW's being beaten, the condition of children after air strikes had taken place in their villages, H & I (harassment and interdiction) fires, and most particularly the command that I received at Khe Sanh that after dark anything was a free fire zone for H & I's. I witnessed the killing of unarmed individuals, destruction of houses, property, crops, the use of prisoners of war as pack animals, the use of CS grenades.

In Operation Hickory, which was within the DMZ, we made an amphibious landing. We were given the order that anything north of the river there, which marked the demarcation line at that point, was to be considered a free fire zone. Well, in Operation Hickory we were told that the reason for our being there was to evacuate Catholic refugees. We had a detachment of military police with my company at that time who were to handle these refugees. After making our landing on about the second or third day, in May of 1967, I went out with the platoon to a village about 1000 meters from our position. From all appearances the villagers had not been notified that they were to be evacuated and, they obviously didn't want to be evacuated. About 30 or 40 villagers were rounded up; they were not given a chance to collect any of their belongings. They were taken back to our position where they were loaded on amtracks and taken down the beach. We were told they were being taken to Gio Linh to the refugee camp. I don't know what actual disposition was made of them after they left our position.

On another occasion, a couple of days later, we saw refugees about 1000 meters in front of our position, moving south. I checked them out with binoculars to see if they were troops or what. They were all people carrying belongings on their back. There were no weapons present. The platoon that I was with at that particular time was in a position about 500 meters from the rest of the company and there were two officers present. Some of the men in the company, or in the platoon, rather, fired upon these refugees. They were too far away for any accurate firing. I don't know if any of them were hit, but there was no command given for them to cease. This went on until they got tired of the sport.

Capt. Ernie Sachs, 1st Marine Division

I entered the Marine Corps in 1964 after working as a news broadcaster for a network radio station. I was a helicopter pilot. I came out as a captain. I was in Vietnam with Marine Medium Helicopter Squadron 362 as a Medivac pilot from August of '66 to September of '67 and my testimony concerns the leveling of villages for no valid reason, throwing Viet Cong suspects from the aircraft after binding and gagging them with copper wire, and racism in the assignment of priorities to medical evacuations where white people were given priority over nonwhite people.

I flew probably 500 Medivac missions in the course of 13 months. I can't recall ever evacuating a Vietnamese civilian. Allied with this there were times at night in bad weather during the monsoon season we would not launch a night Medivac unless it was an emergency. There were instances where a frag would come in; my co-pilot would go out to start the aircraft while I took down the numbers to get to the zone correctly and the major, the operations officer of the squadron, would say, "Now hold it a minute. It's bad weather out there and you're going to get your ass killed and these are only ARVNs.

These aren't Americans. These are gook Marines. Fuck 'em! We don't need 'em. We're not going to risk ourselves for them." We would try to fly the mission anyway. But it was a squadron policy, unwritten, not to launch for gooks if you could possibly avoid it.

Pfc. Robert Craig, 1st Marine Division

I'm 23 years old. I entered the service about two weeks after graduation in 1965. I entered the service after high school in 1965. Went to Vietnam in 1966 to serve with 2nd Battalion, 5th Marines, and served there from September '66 to September '67. When I got out of the service I worked as a laborer.

My testimony basically covers the maltreatment of prisoners, suspects actually, and a convoy running down an old woman with no reason at all—no provocation or anything. And bounties were put on our own men in our own companies if they were inadequate in the field. And they were either disposed of, or wounded, or something to this effect just to make sure they were taken away. The convoy was moving pretty slow and the old woman—like most of the civilians over there sort of ignore the military people going down the road. And it didn't seem like he didn't beep the horn or like do anything, like, he just moved up to the old woman and started nudging her and then I saw her fall out of the way. When the convoy had completely passed, like she was on the road, really like squashed.

Moderator: How many—was it a large convoy?

Craig: No, it was about five trucks, maybe six.

Moderator: Five or six trucks. Did anybody stop from the convoy and see . . . ?

Craig: No, they kept moving. They were loaded.

Moderator: They kept moving. Also, did you ever see the mistreatment of prisoners that we had taken? Viet Cong suspects or NVA?

Craig: Yes, I did. These people were only suspects taken from a village after we had a mine sweep team that was wiped

18

out and I guess people more or less went out to pick up these suspects on a grudge basis. When they brought them back in they were loading them on a truck and they were making a game out of it by grabbing their feet and their hands and swinging them up in the air to see how high they could throw them and land in the back of a duce and a half truck, which had a steel bed.

Moderator: Okay. Were there any senior NCOs present?

Craig: There was a staff sergeant present.

Pvt. Michael Damron, 3rd Marine Division

My age is 24. I'm from Springdale, Arkansas. I was a student before enlisting in the Marines. My rank was private and I served with B Company, 3rd Tank Battalion, 3rd Marine Division, from September 1966 until October 1967. My job was gunner on a tank. I'm presently a student at the University of Arkansas.

In January of 1967 we were on Operation Newcastle about 30 miles out of Da Nang and our function as a tank unit—we had our tank and some infantry people on top of a hill while some more tanks and infantry was sweeping through the valley below—and our job was to more or less plaster the area before the infantry got there and if there was any stragglers left, enemy stragglers, after our people went through, we were to plaster them again. We were told we couldn't fire unless we saw people with packs and rifles. That was more or less the policy as written, but what we made it a practice to do in our unit was to boost the body count. We'd paint a little hat, a triangle-shaped hat, on the side of our tanks for each confirmed kill we had, so any chance we got to add more hats to the side of the tank, we fired. And on this particular occasion we fired on five people that we had no way of knowing who they were because they were not armed.

As far as prisoners of war go, on the back of a tank there's a thing called a travel lock so when the gun tube's to the rear it can be locked down where it won't be bounced around. They don't use these in Vietnam but they use them in the States. But what we used them for in Vietnam was we could put a VC's head or a VC suspect's head in that travel lock and lock it down. But it could be dangerous because if we did hit a bump it could break the person's neck.

Moderator: Mike, you said that this could be done. Was it done and did you witness it?

Damron: Yes, I did.

Moderator: Could you tell us approximately when this was and where?

Damron: This would have been in the same general area, around Da Nang, I believe in Dai Loc province. It would have been in late 1966, around December.

SP/4 Sam Schorr, 20th Brigade

I'm from Los Angeles. I was in the U.S. Army, 86th Combat Engineer Battalion in Vietnam from September 1966 to September 1967, in the area of Lai Khe, the Iron Triangle, the Mekong Delta around Dong Tam, Ben Luc, and Tan An. I was an E-4. That was the highest I ever got; they wouldn't promote me after that. I will testify to the destruction of crops and rice paddies, ripping off graves, random fire on civilians, recon by fire, indiscriminate firing in mad minutes, throwing people out of helicopters, throwing C-rations at kids along the side of the road, killing of water buffaloes, and last but not least, the whole major issue, the issue of fighting in this imperialist war.

Recon by fire is when you go into an area and you're not exactly sure what is in the area. You want to find out, so you just fire into the jungle or into the surrounding vegetation in the hopes you hit the enemy or something. But they really didn't know who was out there or what was out there. And mad minutes is just where everybody on perimeter, around the base camp (you have bunkers all the way around it), opens up and fires away with all their fire power for about a minute, two minutes.

I saw several incidents of recon by fire. This was on con-

20

voy duty. The convoy would stop. Tanks would pull out to the edge of the convoy. These are around inhabited areas; there were villages all up and down the highway. This was Highway 13, Thunder road. And they would point their muzzles down into the vegetation and fire a cannister round. Now a cannister round has something like 7000 oblong bearings in it. It's got a range of about 400 meters and it spreads as it goes. It goes in at an angle. Starts out at a small angle and just goes out like this. It's kind of like a Claymore mine. It just rips everything to pieces that's in the way. If there's anybody out there—any animal, any person, any kid, any hootch—it's going to be destroyed, flattened. Knocks trees to pieces.

Regarding throwing people out of helicopters, I only saw one incident of this. I was coming out to do bunker guard during the day and right outside the perimeter—this was Lai Khe—there was an armored personnel carrier and a Huey chopper, which was warmed up and ready to go. There were people standing around the APC. There were five Vietnamese people. I do not know if they were civilians, Viet Cong, or Viet Cong suspects. Three of them were wounded, had bandages on their bodies and their legs and their arms looked in bad shape. The other two were older men, somewhere around fifty years old. The lieutenant from the armored personnel carrier and the captain from the chopper helped place these people in the helicopter. He got in the helicopter and took off. He got a couple of hundred feet up and three bodies came out. The lieutenant who was on the ground radioed up to the 'copter and he asked, "What happened to the prisoners?" The reply was, point blank, "They tried to escape."

The destruction of crops was fairly widespread. I was in an engineer outfit. I operated a bulldozer and also an earth mover, which is a very large piece of equipment for removing eighteen cubic yards of dirt at a time. When we had to build a base camp or we needed dirt for a road, we just drove off the side of a road into somebody's rice paddy and just started scraping away and taking their dirt. It didn't matter if the Vietnamese people there were using it at the time, or if they were going to use it at a future time. We just went in there

21

and got it anyway 'cause we needed the dirt. Along almost all these rice paddies, they have graves on the dikes, at corners of the dikes, and these are the fathers, mothers, and grand-fathers of the people who lived near that particular rice paddy. If there was a grave in the way, we just went right through it. I scraped up several graves into my pan and probably dumped it on a road somewhere. And there were sergeants and lieutenants watching it. They never said a thing. I was never reprimanded for doing something like this.

Also, this was kind of a contradiction in Army policy. When we were at a base camp that had a rubber plantation in it—this is thousands of rubber trees planted for the use of taking out the sap and using it for latex—when we ripped off a rubber tree we paid the French owner of that plantation 700 piasters per tree. This was the deal they had worked out. Somebody was getting rich off of taking down these unused rubber trees. But when we did it to these local Vietnamese peasants, or anybody living around there, we didn't pay any-body anything. We just went off and did it.

As far as random fire on civilians, this happened quite often, especially on bunker guard. You sit on bunker guard for a week, 24 hours a day, and you get pretty bored. So we'd play little games. The Vietnamese would be working out in their rice paddies with South Vietnamese flags stuck in the rice paddy so you would know they were there. And we would try and knock the flag down. I had a machine gun. My friend had a grenade launcher. We would shoot all over the area and the Vietnamese would just take off for the hills. They thought we were friendly and they put the flag up there to let us know that they were there and we fired at it any-way. This was just out of sheer boredom and also because we just didn't give a damn.

Also, we threw full C-ration cans at kids on the side of the road. Kids would be lined up on the side of the road. They'd be yelling out, "Chop, chop; chop, chop," and they wanted food. They knew we carried C-rations. Well, just for a joke, these guys would take a full can if they were riding shotgun and throw it as hard as they could at a kid's head. I saw several kids' heads split wide open, knocked off the road,

knocked into tires of vehicles behind, and knocked under
tank traps.

SP/4 Dennis Butts, 25th Infantry Division and 9th Infantry Division

I'm from Madison, Wisconsin. I was an infantryman with
the 4th Division and the 9th Division in 1966 and 1967. My
testimony will involve the killing of civilians, the playing of
games with mortars, setting them so that they will burn down
civilian homes, and also I will try to give my insight into why
this happened.

I'm going to talk about the perimeter at Dau Tieng,
which I was on for about two months. I spent about every
night on it. Dau Tieng is on the Michelin rubber plantation
owned by the French. When someone is out there on this
perimeter protecting these rubber trees, well, they might be
just a little bit confused or embittered at what they're doing.
It came down from battalion. We wondered why we weren't
too careful when we were in the rubber about getting mortared, and battalion said the reason we weren't mortared was
because the French were paying a volunteer fee to the Viet
Cong for not mortaring the rubber. Where did the French get
this money? Did they raise their prices on the rubber? No,
they got it from the American government. So the American
government was paying the French rent at Dau Tieng and
then the French were paying the VC. The VC were carrying
out the war in other parts of Vietnam with this money. This
was part of why you might feel a little bit confused in Vietnam at what's going on around you.

I'd like to talk about the general situation on this perimeter. It was really a confusing thing. I don't know if I can
make it clear. We had concertina wire up. The people in the
village were friendly. In these two months I never saw any
sniper fire coming from that village. The girls would come in
at night and stay in the bunkers with us and smoke pot. A lot
of guys would go in the village and sleep in the village at night;
they'd go through the concertina wire. And it was that friendly.

23

Now, the army has a policy of putting people who are in a rear echelon in the perimeters, such as cooks, mechanics, and mortar people (like I was at that time) who have really no experience at combat or anything and might feel a little bit uneasy at what's going on. They put these people on the perimeter, just after they've got off a day of being cook, or working in a motor pool. They're using World War II equipment also, which wasn't designed for Vietnam, so they got 50-caliber machine guns for the mess halls. Well, the mess halls don't really need 50-calibers so they put them out in this perimeter. Now the perimeter of the village was about 150 to 200 feet from this 50-caliber. And anybody who knows what a 50-caliber can do—if he can see any logic in that, I would like to know.

But, anyway, they got this 50-caliber sitting there and the bullets on a 50-caliber are about that long [approximately six inches]. With some guys, not everyone, it just got to be a game of shooting at lights in the village. One night there was a light or something in the village, and this one guy, he was from a rear echelon, a mechanic, he was on this 50-caliber. He saw something and he opened up onto the village with a 50-caliber in about a ten-second burst. Then the rest of the perimeter opened up. Not everyone, but a lot of firing. And all I could hear—it was just people screaming all of a sudden; people screaming, you know. So a few guys started yelling, "Come on, cut it out. Cut it out!" And everybody was wondering what was going on because there was no fire coming from the village. Then there was a big silence, and all of a sudden, just babies crying. And, you know, it just—everytime I hear a baby cry right now, I—that comes back to me.

In another incident that happened, at the same perimeter, up about 100 yards, and this gives a little bit more insight into why this thing happened. They had a man whom I knew. He wasn't a close friend, but I'd known him pretty well. And he just didn't want to be in Vietnam. He started out to be pretty straight, a pretty straight guy, pretty level-headed. He tried everything to get out of the army. He took court-martials and Article 15s and he finally shot himself in the foot to get out of the army. They patched up his foot and sent him on this perim. He was on the perim and there were a couple of other guys there with him. I was on the next bunker and we had field phones in between us. There was a kid out there urinating. And this guy talked the other two and himself into shooting. Now, I think the other two guys shot. It was only about 150 feet away. I don't think they tried to hit him. But this guy did with a grenade launcher. They hit him with this grenade launcher and I don't know, he must have been about 13 to 15 years old. I witnessed this. We went into the village and he had shrapnel in his back. The medics did treat him and take him into the first aid station.

This guy did not get a reprimand for this. He was just kind of given up on and he was still put in the field again. I don't know whatever happened to him, after that. But, I'm just trying to say the things that happen to people. They go in the army pretty sane or level-headed or adjusted. They tell the army that maybe they shouldn't be there and nobody listens. They just put them in a worse situation and this is how some of these things happen.

L/Cpl. Thomas Heidtman, 1st Marine Division

I'm from Ann Arbor, Michigan. I served from October '66 to September '67; I served with Third Battalion, 5th Marines, all this time. I can attest to prisoners being shot. I've seen it; I've done it. Villages being burned was a common everyday thing in the "Burning 5th Marines." Prisoners were tortured. They were forced to carry other wounded prisoners on bamboo poles for up to seven hours. Women and children were brutalized. I've seen water buffaloes killed. Any time you have to dig a hole, you find a nice soft bean field. You destroy crops. Rice is contaminated with CS. For three months they were attempting to burn rice with illumination grenades, which never did work, but they kept on trying. Destroying villages was a common practice. On one occasion a captain ordered the burning of a ville because we were staying in this area for a day and a half and it was "too close."

My first day, I was informed that the nickname of the

25

company was the "Burning 5th Marines." Once, just before my first operation, we had a company formation, which means that the entire company who was going on the operation is fully equipped with everything they're going to take with them, including ammunition. At the time, our company commander was a 1st lieutenant, who was hit on Hill 110 in April, but he said that we're going out in the morning and we're going out on choppers. We're going out into an area west of Tam Ky. Then he said, "We're going to have a Zippo inspection right now." And I would say approximately two-thirds of the entire company had Zippo lighters. We held them up, lit them, demonstrated that they were filled, would burn. Then put them away. He smiled and let it go at that. When we went out, I would say 50 percent at least of the villages we passed through would be burned to the ground. There was no difference between the ones we burned and the ones we didn't burn. It was just that where we had time, we burned them.

I've seen a gunnery sergeant take a 45 and kill six piglets that probably came from Americans because they had a big program to give the Vietnamese people pigs, ducks, and things like that. They were shot because their area, their pan, or whatever, was right next to a village or a hootch that was burning. The entire village, for about a quarter of a mile, was on fire with illumination grenades or Zippo lighters. Everything was burned. Everything was torn down. All the animals were killed. Water buffaloes were shot and allowed to just lay right where they were. They were just shot right in their pan; they couldn't move. It's hard to kill a water buffalo, but when he's standing right there, there's nothing much he can do. Everything is burned.

On one particular occasion we had been moving on Operation Arizona, in April and May; we'd been moving constantly. About one hour just before dark, the order came right from our 1st lieutenant to 1st squad, which I was a member of, to go burn the village because it's too close. We're spending too much time here. So my squad, myself included, went and put a Zippo lighter to the village. Burned it. They were still inside the houses. They came outside and just stood there and cried and carried on. A short while later they wandered off. We don't know what happened to them. That was the only village in the immediate vicinity, so we cleared the area, more or less.

Everything was liable to be burned or destroyed. We would stop along the side of a hill, going up a hill, just to check out the top, which is a procedure the Marine Corps seems to adhere to. Every time we would stop somebody would be taking a machete or some such thing and chopping down banana trees. The people would slice potatoes and dry them out in front of their hootches. These would be scattered all over the place. They would just be kicked and destroyed. Men would urinate on these vegetables that were drying in the sun. If they complained, they were definitely brutalized. That was a common procedure.

The reason I came down here was because I've been living with this thing for two and a half years. There was an aura of hate in my outfit. I mean, a Vietnamese—there was no such thing to my unit as a friendly Vietnamese. Every Vietnamese was a gook. I've hardly ever heard the term Vietnamese. They were always gooks. There was no difference between a good one and a bad one except that the good one at the time is carrying no weapon, but he's still fair game.

The games that some of the Marines in my outfit played, myself included, would be to find older papa-sans with long whiskers, which I guess is the symbol of his identity in their culture, and they would just be cut. Every man in my outfit had a least a combat knife and they would just cut these whiskers. They would brutalize anybody who complained. We would move into a village and we would just sit down. We owned the village while we were there. These people would do what we told them, or they wouldn't be allowed to stay in their own house, or would be beaten inside the house.

In one village we were using this particular hootch for the command post. There were officers, two officers and two senior enlisted men inside. The old grandfather appeared to be about 60 or 70 years old. He would not cooperate and go get water for some of the enlisted men and officers, so he was picked up by two marines; each had a wrist and an ankle and

27

they just pitched him about 15 feet out the back door; he just landed there and split.

To the Marines, there was no such thing as a free fire zone in my outfit. Every place was a free fire zone, whether it was 50 yards from the perimeter or five miles or whatever. One other thing that was more or less like a joke, like cutting the whiskers off, and it would get a laugh every time from somebody, was if we were moving through a village and there was a woman present. Her clothes, at least the top half of her clothes were just ripped. I've seen that happen, and done it several times, probably thirty, forty times I've seen civilians with their clothes just—just because they were female and they were old enough for somebody to get a laugh at—their clothes, the top of their clothes, at least, would be ripped. Just torn right down. It only takes one hand to rip those kind of clothing. They're real thin silk or whatever, and they would be shoved out into the ditch and we'd just keep going.

Sgt. Michael McCusker, 1st Marine Division

I'm from Portland, Oregon. I was in the 1st Marine Division, in I Corps, in 1966 and 1967. I was discharged on 19th October 1967 as a Sergeant E-5. This ragged piece of paper here is a Xeroxed copy of my discharge papers. I was in the 1st Marine Division with the Informational Services Office, which meant that I was an infantry reporter-photographer. I spent all of my time out in the field with the infantry on infantry operations. I went out with damned near every Marine outfit in all of I Corps from 1st Marine Division and 3rd Marine Division units. And so, these things in the field, the torturing of prisoners, the use of scout dogs in this torture, the "Bell Telephone Hour" with the field phones—by seeing all of these units, I discovered that no one unit was any worse than another. That this was standard procedure. That it was almost like watching the same film strip continually, time after time after time. Within every unit there was the same prejudice; there was the same bigotry toward Vietnamese. All Vietnamese.

28

I just want to mention a few atrocities of a larger scale that I saw. All three of them were ironically with the same battalion—1st Battalion, 5th Marine Regiment, 1st Marine Division. All three atrocities happened in the month of September and October 1966. Now the first one took place around September 6th or 7th, 1966, about ten miles northwest of the province capital of Tam Ky, near the mountains. It was in a pineapple forest and a Marine had just been killed. He had been hit by a sniper and the entire battalion, in revenge, destroyed two entire villages, wiping out everything living, the people (and that was men, women, their children), all their livestock, burning the huts, destroying the paddies, their gardens, their hedgerows, just wiped them out—erased them. They did not exist the moment after the Marines were finished and they might never have existed.

The next instance happened also in the same month of September when a squad of nine men, that was a Chu Lai rifle squad, went into this village. They were supposed to go after what they called a Viet Cong whore. They went into the village and instead of capturing her, they raped her—every man raped her. As a matter of fact, one man said to me later that it was the first time he had ever made love to a woman with his boots on. The man who led the platoon, or the squad, was actually a private. The squad leader was a sergeant but he was a useless person and he let the private take over his squad. Later he said he took no part in the raid. It was against his morals. So instead of telling his squad not to do it, because they wouldn't listen to him anyway, the sergeant went into another side of the village and just sat and stared bleakly at the ground, feeling sorry for himself. But at any rate, they raped the girl, and then, the last man to make love to her, shot her in the head.

They then rounded up ten villagers, put 'em in a hut (I don't know how they killed them—grenaded them or shot 'em down), and burned the hut. They came back to the company area where it was bivouacked for the night while on a regular routine search and destroy mission. I personally came into contact with this when the squad came back, told their CO, who was a lieutenant, and they hastily set back off again towards that village with the lieutenant. I sort of tagged along in the rear and when I got up there they were distributing these bodies that were charred and burned and I asked what these bodies were. They said, "Oh, we were hit by an ambush. These were the people who ambushed, but we got 'em." Okay, I didn't want to ask them how they killed them because all the bodies were burned as if they'd been roasted on a spit.

There was a tiny little form, that of a child, lying out in the field with straw over its face. It had been clubbed to death. As later was brought out, the Marine that clubbed the child to death didn't really want to look at the child's face so he put straw over it before he clubbed it. The woman survived, somehow, and crawled to a neighbor; the neighbor ran off to the ARVN commanders. The commanders were rather angry, put pressure on the Marine Corps, and these men were tried. However, they got very light sentences—a little slap on the wrist. I don't know exactly how much time they got nor do I know how much time they actually served, but they're on the streets again because I ran into one about two years ago in New York.

The third atrocity was a village called Duc Pho, which was farther northwest of Tam Ky, across the first range of mountains into several valleys. This area was not touched for two years until the Army started taking up operations in that area. Jonathan Shell wrote a very, very graphic two-part story for the *New Yorker* concerning that area, mentioning that nobody had been in there for two years after the Marines had passed through. Nobody had to. There wasn't really much left after we went through. In this one particular village of Duc Pho, another man was killed by a sniper. This involved Bravo Company, 1st Battalion, 5th Marines, and I believe it was the 1st Platoon with the company commander along. Well, the CO pulled us back. We were sweeping across the paddy when this sergeant got hit. He pulled us back and called in for nape, which is napalm, or which the military now likes to refer to as incinder jell, as if it were as harmless as Jello, an after-dinner dessert. But it was napalm.

We walked into the ville after the fires burned down and

there was an old man lying on a cot, burned to death with his hands stiff in rigor mortis, reaching for the sky as if in prayer or supplication forgiving us for what we had done. We walked past him and across the hedgerow there was an old woman lying dead curled into the fetal position as if she had been just born. An old man lay beside her. Over the next hedgerow there were 30 dead children. They had been lying out there in this courtyard for us to see them before we got into that village. They were laid out there by survivors, who split into the jungle. Now these kids, 30 of them, none were over fifteen; some of them were babies. Some looked like they had just been sunburned, that was all. Their skins were a very ruddy, ruddy pink or scarlet color. Others were just charred with their guts hanging out. Ironically it was my mother's birthday, 27 October, and I somehow seemed to feel that these were her children.

An officer, a captain, walked up to me and said, "Well, Sgt. McCusker,"—remember I was the reporter—"Do you see what the Viet Cong did to their own people?" And I said, "Captain, I saw our planes drop the napalm." He says, "Well, Sgt. McCusker, you had better write that the Viet Cong did it." I told the captain politely what I thought he should do to himself and I walked off. Now these things happened. Now these were some of the more gruesome things that happened, or more gruesome because of the numbers. But daily things like this happened—a kid shot down in the paddy because, well, it looked like an adult running away. I couldn't see, so we walk up to him, and it's a kid. The philosophy was that anybody running must be a Viet Cong; he must have something to hide or else he would stick around for the Americans, not taking into consideration that he was running from the Americans because they were continually shooting at him. So they shot down anybody who was running.

I was in a helicopter once and I saw this farmer in a cart. Suddenly the farmer in the cart just blew into all sorts of pieces and the helicopter I was in was shaking like the devil. It wasn't hard to put it together because I watched the gunner finish off the rounds. He had extra ammo.

The tortures started in the villages. Prisoners were picked

31

up by the average infantryman, who really didn't have much idea of exactly what intelligence was needed. So, therefore, you're all prisoners. We'll let interrogators take care of it. The method of taking prisoners was that you take the villagers that were left in the village, not those that had run away. You tied them to a tree and got the dog handler to let the dog jump and bite at the person tied to the tree. Or again, with the field telephone, you wired it up to his ears, his nose, his genitals. This was done to women—I've seen it done to women. In Ben Song, which was the province capital, in a prison, this guy was telling me all about why war was hell. He took me down to this dungeon where South Vietnamese troops were pulling fingernails out of an old woman. There was an American captain standing by, rocking on his heels, rather enjoying the show.

I could testify to the systematic destruction of village hospitals, by mortars, by air, by artillery, believing that if these hospitals were destroyed the Viet Cong could not use them for their wounded. I was also on an operation in the Rung Sat area just north of Saigon, which is just mud flats, like the Mississippi delta at high water. It was in April 1966, with the 1st Battalion, 5th Marines again. They were a battalion landing team at that time. We came across a big NLF hospital complex and destroyed it out of hand. Now interestingly enough, in Portland, Oregon, where I was a medic in the student strike, we had an unauthorized hospital tent in what was called the park blocks out in front of the college. The city decided to destroy it because it was an unauthorized hospital. We did have patients in it, but these were unauthorized people too. They were long-hairs. So the cops came in, the tactical squad with their sticks. They bloodied up about 30 of us pretty badly and did a lot more damage to perhaps 50 more. So not only in Vietnam do Americans destroy hospitals. It was graphically pointed out to the people in Portland that they were destroyed, too, by police power—except of course, the hospital was not officially authorized. Nor are Vietnamese hospitals in the villages.

Doctor Margarette, who was in Quang Ngai, can testify to the condition of the provincial hospital in Quang Ngai, the

Vietnamese hospital for the province. That hospital is so damned overcrowded that they can't get anything done. People are dying in those wards; they just shove them off the beds and put somebody else on them. One of the reasons that that damn hospital is so crowded is because all the little hospitals within the villages were all destroyed.

Quang Ngai, in that province of Quang Ngai, an entire war of attrition is being put across there. My Lai is in Quang Ngai; My Lai suffered that war of attrition. When Calley and his people went through there, it was not the first time anyone went through My Lai and put the torch to it, nor was it the last time. You can prove it by a Reuters dispatch of October 1969. They were doing it again, and in the villages of the whole Son My province. The entire Quang Ngai area was slated for destruction. The Vietnamese were slated for relocation and forced urbanization—which is what is happening in this country as a matter of fact. So the methods don't differ.

I guess, really, that's the end of my testimony except right now, while I'm speaking, it's happening in all of Southeast Asia; some guys are going through what I did, what all of us did; they are going through it right now. The Vietnamese, Cambodians, and Laotians are dying right now, at this exact moment, and they will continue to die tomorrow, maybe even next year.

Cpl. Paul Olimpieri, 1st Marine Division

I entered the Marine Corps about nine months after graduating high school. I was in 1st Battalion, 5th Marines in Vietnam and my testimony is on killing civilians and killing livestock and destroying villages.

We were in a sweep in a rice paddy and the flank man spotted somebody and told him to halt and he started running and I fired an M-79 over the trees. It went off and the man went down and our lieutenant told us to go over there and check and see if he had an ID and find out if he was dead or what was happening with him. We went over there and he was still alive. He was about 70 years old. I believe he was some sort of religious, like a monk or something like that from his dress. He had an ID card and he was in pretty bad shape, so they didn't want to call in a Medivac chopper, so they told us to kill him. And the person who did the killing fired about six rounds in him and I had to tell him to stop. Right after that we told the lieutenant what the situation was and he called in and said, "Get rid of the—." He told us to get rid of the ID card before we killed him. He called in one VC body count.

Moderator: So this man who was killed wasn't even a suspect. He was civilian.

Olimpieri: Right. He didn't halt when he was told so they shot him.

Pfc. Bill Perry, 101st Airborne Division

I served in Vietnam from '67 to '68.

On March 5th, 1968, in the province of Phuc Long, village of Song Be, a platoon of us, 29 of us, were on a search and destroy mission. A few of us who were considered expendable were told to walk point. As we came up out of a bamboo thicket into a clearing, a woman with whom I and one of the other two people had previously had what you might call business transactions with concerning marijuana, informed us of an imminent ambush on the part of the local forces. Myself and two others ran into her home with her. We weren't sure whether she was bullshitting us or what, but we were scared so we ran into her home. The rest of the platoon came up out of the valley into the clearing and was ambushed. We were isolated pretty well from the rest of the platoon while they were getting shot up. And when an NCO came up to look into the house where we were kind of looking out the door with the woman, the NCO automatically figured that we must be VC prisoners and he shot her up. She had a very young child inside her bomb shelter. Every Vietnamese home has to have a bomb shelter. The ambush actually lasted about two or three minutes, and the platoon got pretty well shot up. For about five hours they called in artillery and air strikes and pretty well demolished the town of Song Be. Finally when enough reinforcements came, they went out to sweep the area. They decided to throw fragmentation, or white phosphorous grenades, inside of each bunker regardless of what was going down in any bunker. We tried to stop them from fragging other bunkers where we could hear screams or moans or whatever, but they were really into it.

There was another incident in mid-July 1968 in the vicinity of Nui Ba Den where we had been in about two days of steady combat. We had found a lot of bodies, some killed by air strikes and some killed by small arms fire. And the military fear, you know, came through once again in their mutilation of bodies. They were very much into cutting patches and numbers on dead bodies in this particular incident. I could go on with more horror stories, but like, we all know what happens.

Moderator: You mentioned something before about an order received by the higher up and crossing across the national borders. Could you mention something on that?

Perry: It was very well known that we were within two clicks of Cambodia, which is about a mile and two-tenths. Very often we went on search and destroy missions directly west as far as 8 to 10 clicks and back. We were definitely going into Cambodia.

Moderator: Did you ever make contact in Cambodia? Did you ever make contact when you crossed the border?

Perry: No, I didn't.

S/Sgt. Jack Smith, 3rd Marine Division

I'm 27 years old. I was a student at the University of Connecticut for 3½ years before I enlisted in the Marine Corps in 1966 and I was also an unemployed carpenter at the time I enlisted. I was a Counter-Mortar Radar Team Chief and a Vietnamese interpreter. I served in Vietnam in 1967 and all of 1969. I was with Headquarters Battery, 12th Marines, and I am presently an unemployed carpenter and an on-strike student. My testimony concerns genocide against the Vietnamese people, murder of civilians—old women and children—harassment and maltreatment of children, and also the murder of children; the maltreatment of ARVN soldiers; racism against the blacks both institutional and by official policy and individual; the crossing of borders with artillery fire, and the maltreatment of POWs.

As far as the POWs go, our radar location was located right next to the heliport at Charley Two, which was overlooking the DMZ up by Con Thien. They'd bring the prisoners in from the field and some of them severely wounded and crying for water. They were always denied medical aid, food, and water until after they had testified to what we wanted to have them testify to. I myself didn't interrogate them. We simply stood out there and watched them and then they would take several of the Vietnamese—they might have four or five prisoners—they'd throw four or five of them along inside the chopper. The chopper would take off, fly over up by the DMZ, come back about 10 or 15 minutes later and unload two. Somehow, along the line, somebody had decided they were going to take a walk out there so they suddenly lost a couple of prisoners, but we never questioned this. If you questioned it, it was simply—they were just gooks anyway so it didn't matter.

I had three radar locations up along the DMZ there, about forty people there, and we had to make a run in with our vehicle every week or every day into the supply base at Dong Ha. So we'd send our truck into Dong Ha every day and we'd have to pass through the village of Cam Lo, which was just a civilian village located on the way to Highway 9, which runs into Dong Ha. Every day as we passed through the village—the GIs, when they originally get in country they feel very friendly toward the Vietnamese and they like to toss candy at the kids, but as they become hardened to it and kind of embittered against the war, as you drive through the ville you take the cans of C-rats and the cases and you peg 'em at the kids; you try to belt them over the head. And one of the fun games that always went was you dropped the C-rats cans or the candy off the back of your truck just so that

36

the kid will have time to dash out, grab the candy, and get run over by the next truck. One of the other fun games was you take the candy and you toss it out on a concertina wire. The kids are so much dying for the candy that they'll tear their flesh and their clothing and their clothes off trying to get at this candy which you've thrown inside the barbed wire.

Additionally, when we had to go into Dong Ha we also used to have to make a garbage run about every other day and the garbage dump was located just down the road in front of the village of Cam Lo. In order to unload our garbage with the least amount of harassment to the Americans what we would do is send down our barrels of garbage, we'd send down a team of five or six or a squad of five or six Marines along with it. One guy would be assigned to dump the garbage and the other six would beat the Vietnamese, shoot them, do anything they could to keep them off the truck while you were unloading the garbage because they wanted to get into the cans and be the first ones to scrounge through and get something to eat. So in order to save your vehicle and keep the equipment that you had on it, you'd just throw the Vietnamese off the side of the truck and dump the garbage cans on top of them—just chuck 'em overboard.

SP/5 James Duffy, 1st Air Cavalry Division

I served as a machine gunner on a CH-47, Chinook helicopter with Company A, 228th Aviation Battalion, 1st Air Cav Division, from February '67 to April '68.

Most of our missions we flew alone and we had a wide variety of missions. One such mission was a gas run where we loaded the ship with twelve 55-gallon drums of what I was told was CS gas, which we dropped into a well traveled path in the An Lo Valley. We were told that gas would be effective for a number of weeks; it would remain there. Another mission was a defoliation run on our own perimeter in An Khe— that was the base camp at the time. The perimeter was occupied by GIs, grunts, pulling guard duty, and also Vietnamese civilians from the neighboring town who were allowed to chop wood there. So both our people and theirs were exposed to the defoliants. And when I first became a gunner, I was told the company policy was to return fire from all guns when fired on. To continue fire until our supply of ammo had been expended. This was usually thousand-round belts that we kept in each of the two M-60 machine guns. Also the crew chief, myself, and the flight engineer had M-16s with as much ammunition as we wished to fire.

It was quite usual that there would be a sniper outside a village in the foliage, in the trees, and if we took fire from one sniper we'd return fire on that sniper and then continue to spray the entire village with machine gun fire and M-16 ammunition until we either ran out of ammunition or we had flown so far away from the village that we could no longer reach them with the weapons. Now, the thousand-round belts we used in the machine guns were usually straight tracer rounds, so during the dry season (when the Vietnamese live in these hootches made of C-ration cans and straw huts) the tracers would set fire to the huts so the ones that we didn't get with ammunition we could try and burn them out. The freefire zones were posted on the operation map in the operations tent and this gave us a policy to kill anything that moved within that area.

On one operation, I was flying an LZ. We took fire when a round hit one of our fuel pods; and one of the jobs of a crew member is also to pull maintenance on the ship—and the more maintenance you have to pull the less flying time and the less chance you get to kill gooks, because that's the mental attitude that the Army forces you into. So we were kind of mad that we had taken a round in the fuel pod, so after leaving the LZ we requested the pilot fly over the area we had taken the round from so we could get whoever it was that had fired at us. We were all pretty uptight about it, and as soon as we left the LZ, I noticed a contingent of Vietnamese peasants chopping wood and I decided, well, if the Vietnamese can fire a round into my ship, then I can fire as many rounds into the Vietnamese as I want to. So I swung my machine gun onto this group of peasants and opened fire.

Fortunately, the gun jammed after one or two rounds, which was pretty lucky, because this group of peasants turned out to be a work party hired by the government to clear the area and there were GIs guarding them about 50 meters away. But my mind was so psyched out into killing gooks that I never even paid attention to look around and see where I was. I just saw gooks and I wanted to kill them. I was pretty scared after that happened because that sort of violated the unwritten code that you can do anything you want to as long as you don't get caught. That's—I guess that's what happened with the My Lai incident. Those guys just were following the same pattern that we've been doing there for ten years, but they had the misfortune of getting caught at it.

And rotor wash from the helicopters was a very effective and sadistic weapon. Chinook helicopter is basically a cargo ship; that's what it's designed for. I forget the weight you can pick up with one, but when you've got a full load, you can put out a rotor wash at certain times that approaches a hundred miles an hour. Some of the things we used to like to do was in the morning the people from hamlets and villages go out to a designated field to defecate and if we'd be on an early morning mission, we'd spot them, make a swoop in, and we could get up to 120 knots—about 130 miles an hour. And as you swoop in with the ship, just as you approach, the pilot would flair the ship on its tail, and the rotor wash would spin around and hit the people, blowing them over through the sand and their defecation. This was one of the things that we did for kicks.

Rotor wash was also used to blow down the huts—literally blow down the villages; like I said they are made out of straw and junk. So we'd come in and flair on a ship and just blow away a person's house. Also, the Vietnamese, when they've harvested a crop of rice, put it out on these large pans to dry and that harvest is what is supposed to maintain them for that season—what they're supposed to live on. We'd come in, flair the ship, and let the rotor wash blow the rice, blow their entire supply of food for that harvest over a large area. And then laugh as we'd watch them running around trying to pick up individual pieces of rice out of a rice paddy. Over an area larger than this room.

It was also used to spook water buffalo. The Vietnamese when they plow their fields and rice paddies they follow the rows of plants which are fairly straight. And if we'd spot somebody plowing his field, we'd make a run on him. That would spook the water buffalo and the water buffalo would take off in any old direction with that plow ripping up the field and usually the farmer being dragged with the plow through the field.

Once we were picking up a sling load of ammunition and the Army had a habit of putting pick-up zones and drop-off zones right near well traveled roads, you know, roads traveled by the local villages. So we were hovering over this sling load of, I think it was howitzer rounds, and I was hanging out the window observing what appeared to be a 12-year-old Vietnamese boy standing there watching us. And as we lifted up with the load, the rotor wash increased because of the weight and it blew him into the path of a 2½ ton truck with trailer, which killed him instantly.

The psychological effect is something I'd like to bring out here to you people. When that happened, my first reaction, and my flight engineer who was observing this too, our first reaction was, I guess, you would call normal. It would be horror, pain, and then I realized that I caught myself immediately and I said, "No, you can't do that," because you develop a shell while you are in the military. They brainwash you. They, they take all the humanness out of you and you develop this crust which enables you to survive in Vietnam. And if you let that protective shell down, even for a second, it could mean—it's the difference between you flipping out or managing to make it through. And I caught myself letting the shell down and I, and I, tightened up right away. And started laughing about it and joking about it with the flight engineer. He sort of moved on the same logic because I guess he thought it sort of knocked his shell down too.

When we picked up POWs to transfer them to a POW camp, they'd be blindfolded and their hands would usually be tied behind their backs. On a few occasions, not often, I and other people would pistol whip them with our 45s and

40

when that wasn't cool to do, because maybe we had a, you know, somebody flying the ship that really wasn't hip to how to off the gooks, then we'd kick them around as we walked around the ship. Also, on the ship, when we hit the LZ at times, we'd drop the ramp down half-way and, like I said, these people are blindfolded and tied, and we walked them off the ramp and it was literally like walking off this table, blindfolded with your hands tied. So they'd just fall flat on their faces.

Also, during test flights, we'd go to a specific area where the pilots could check out the controls and this would attract a lot of Vietnamese. We'd throw out the C-ration cans that we didn't like and, after they thought they were getting a lot of food, we'd hand them cans of 5606, which is helicopter hydraulic fluid and very poisonous. And I observed one kid, that I handed a can of hydraulic fluid, take a good healthy drink out of it before his mother knocked it over, knocked it right out of his hand, and he was immediately sick right after that happened.

In one incident we were flying back from Khe Sanh Valley and we took fire from six NVA, which caused the ship to explode in the air and make a crash landing. Now, on the way down, because our company policy was to just keep on firing, I had fired at all the military targets I could spot and I looked out across the field and I spotted a Vietnamese woman peasant running away from the ship. I fired a burst of about six or seven rounds into her back before we flamed, before we hit the ground. When I was being questioned as to what happened about two weeks later by a captain in my company, I told him what we did and what I did. We both had a good laugh about it. That was pretty much company policy.

Also in Hue, during the Tet Offensive in '68, I observed American fighters and bombers (Phantoms) dropping bombs and napalm into very crowded streets full of civilians. I don't know how many people were wiped out in that place. They blamed that on the NVA. Also, I was flying tail gun at the time on one mission into Hue, and just for kicks, the pilot told me to spray a house with my M-16. I don't know if the house was occupied, but the area was occupied by civilians. This was common policy. Kill anything you want to kill, any time you want to kill it—just don't get caught.

SP/4 Carl Rippberger, 9th Infantry Division

I'm 23, I was a student before I entered the service. I was in Vietnam from May of 67 to May of 68. I was in K troop, 3rd Squadron, 11th Armored Cavalry Regiment. I was a machine gunner for the first few months I was there. Later on I drove an armored cavalry assault vehicle. I'm now a salesman for an electrical distributor.

In June or July of '67 our armored column moved into a village. The people obviously heard us coming and fled the village in fear of what would happen if they were still there when we got there. We made a thorough search of the village. We found no weapons and nothing to suspect that these people were Viet Cong. Orders came down to burn the village anyway. It was a small farming village of maybe 10 to 15 hootches. All the people's belongings, everything they owned were in these hootches.

We were on search and destroy and we were just driving through. The helicopter spotted this small farming village and as we moved in, the tanks and armored cavalry assault vehicles were very loud. They can be heard for miles and the people left before we got there. We found no weapons or anything there. I don't know where the people would have gone, other than into the jungle waiting for us to leave.

Sgt. Jamie Henry, 4th Infantry Division

I'm 23 years old. I was drafted on March 8, 1967. ETS'd March 7, 1969. Entered Vietnam August 31, 1967 and returned to the United States in August 1968. I'll be testifying on the murder of innocent civilians, which ultimately culminated in the execution of 19 women and children and the causes behind these murders.

Okay, what I have to say is a direct result of the policy by the United States Army in Vietnam, and what I'm going to detail was reported to the United States Army CID. I made a full statement to them. I gave names, dates, grid coordinates, etc., etc., etc. We have my signing of the statement on film with the two CID agents, who are really assholes, but we have it on film so they can't deny it and it's witnessed, etc., etc., etc. So there's no way that they can deny this. This statement was given to the CID over a year ago, almost exactly a year ago, and I'm sure they'll come out with something to say about it—why they haven't done anything about it. They'll probably say it's a lie, but it has been corroborated. I just want to give a brief account of what happened.

On August 8th our company executed a 10-year-old boy. We shot him in the back with a full magazine M-16. Approximately August 16th to August 20th—I'm not sure of the date—a man was taken out of his hootch sleeping, was put into a cave, and he was used for target practice by a lieutenant, the same lieutenant who had ordered the boy killed. Now they used him for target practice with an M-60, an M-16, and a 45. After they had pretty well shot him up with the 60, they backed off aways to see how good a shot they were with a 45 because it's such a lousy pistol. By this time he was dead.

On February 8th—this was after a fire fight and we had lost eight men—on February 8th, we found a man in a spider hole. He was of military age. He spoke no English, of course. We did not have an interrogator, which was one of the problems in the field. He was asked if he were VC and, of course, he kept denying it. "No VC, no VC." He was held down under an APC and he was run over twice—the first time didn't kill him.

About an hour later we moved into a small hamlet, this was in I Corps, it was in a Marine AO. We moved into a small hamlet, 19 women and children were rounded up as VCS (Viet Cong Suspects) and the lieutenant that rounded them up called the captain on the radio and he asked what should be done with them. The captain simply repeated the order that came down from the colonel that morning. The order

43

that came down from the colonel that morning was to kill anything that moves, which you can take anyway you want to take it. When the captain told the lieutenant this, the lieutenant rang off. I got up and I started walking over to the captain thinking that the lieutenant just might do it because I had served in his platoon for a long time. As I started over there, I think the captain panicked—he thought the lieutenant might do it too, and this was a little more atrocious than the other executions that our company had participated in, only because of the numbers. But the captain tried to call him up, tried to get him back on the horn, and he couldn't get a hold of him. As I was walking over to him, I turned, and I looked in the area. I looked toward where the supposed VCS were, and two men were leading a young girl, approximately 19 years old, very pretty, out of a hootch. She had no clothes on so I assumed she had been raped, which was pretty SOP, and she was thrown onto the pile of the 19 women and children, and five men around the circle opened up on full automatic with their M-16s. And that was the end of that.

Now there was a lieutenant who heard this over the radio in our company—he had stayed back with some mortars—he, when we got back to our night location, he was going halfway out of his mind because he had just gotten there, relatively. He was one of these—I don't know, I guess he was naive or something, believed in the old American ideal. He was going nuts. He was going to report it to everybody. After that day he calmed down and the next day he didn't say anything about it. We got in a wretched fire fight the next day and the whole thing was just sort of lost in the intensity of the war.

I don't want to go into the details of these executions because the executions are the direct result of a policy. It's the policy that is important. The executions are secondary because the executions are created by the policy that is, I believe, a conscious policy within the military. Number one, the racism in the military is so rampant. Now you have all heard of the military racism. It's institutionalized; it is policy; it is SOP; you are trained to be a racist. When you go into basic training, you are taught that the Vietnamese are not

44

people. You are taught they are gooks and all you hear is "gook, gook, gook, gook." And once you take the Vietnamese people, or any of the Asian people, because the Asian serviceman in Vietnam is the brunt of the same racism because the GIs over there do not distinguish one Asian from another. They are trained so thoroughly that all Asians become the brunt of this racism.

You are trained "gook, gook, gook," and once the military has got the idea implanted in your mind that these people are not humans, they are subhuman, it makes it a little bit easier to kill 'em. One barrier is removed, and this is intentional, because obviously, the purpose of the military is to kill people. And if you're not an effective killer, they don't want you. The military doesn't distinguish between North Vietnamese, South Vietnamese, Viet Cong, civilian—all of them are gooks, all of them are considered to be subhuman. None of them are any good, etc. And all of them can be killed and most of them are killed.

Now the second reason for atrocities that occur is because it doesn't take very long for an infantryman in the field to realize that he is fighting for nobody's freedom. You can ask any of the men here. They may have thought they were fighting to protect their mother when they got there, but they sure didn't believe that very long. And this isn't just the grunt. It's the lieutenants, it's the officers in the field. Our captain believed it.

It takes only a few months to be subjugated to the circumstances of Vietnam when you come to the realization that you are not fighting for Ky's freedom; you are not fighting for Thieu's freedom; you are not fighting for your mother's freedom or anybody's freedom. You're just getting your asses shot up and all you want to do is go home.

SP/4 Joe Galbally, Americal Division

I'm 23, I served as a Pfc in the 198th Light Infantry Brigade from October of '67 to April of '68 when I was Medivac'd to Japan. My testimony will deal with the gassing of

45

hungry children, the use of scout dogs on innocent civilians, indiscriminate leveling of villages, killing of livestock, and pollution of water supply. In other words, they made it totally impossible for these people to live in their ancestral homelands again.

I'll talk about the rape first. As I said earlier, I was a Pfc in an infantry company, which meant that there was about 75 of us turned loose on the civilian population in Vietnam. We would set up our night perimeter between three and four every evening. If we had passed any villages on the way to this night perimeter, there would be patrols mounted and sent out. On several occasions, one in particular, we set up on a hill which was strategically important, I suppose. There was a village sitting at the bottom of the hill. We went back down to the village; it was about an eight man patrol. We entered a hootch. These people are aware of what American soldiers do to them, so naturally they tried to hide the young girls. We found one hiding in a bomb shelter in sort of the basement of her house. She was taken out, raped by six or seven people in front of her family, in front of us, and the villagers. This wasn't just one incident; this was just the first one I can remember. I know of 10 or 15 of such incidents at least.

Moderator: Joe, you told me about a guy who collected ID cards. Do you want to talk about that?

Galbally: Okay. There was an individual, I won't mention his name, he was a friend of mine, a Spec/4, and he was, I guess you would say, the platoon hatchet man. Any time that he had a prisoner that nobody in the room wanted, this guy would take his ID card and tell him to "Di Di Mau," which is "run" in Vietnamese. The guy would get about ten feet, and get a full burst of automatic, which is 20 rounds, in the back. As I said, I was Medivac in April of '68 and as of April I know that he had at least five or six ID cards also. He was, I guess, more or less proud of the fact that he was the hatchet man and was all the time showing everybody the ID cards. "Look where I got this guy and, how about this, and look at this." It was common knowledge what was going on. On certain occasions, if there was something that had to be done, the commanding officer would call up and ask for this

46

guy, by name, over the battalion radio. I'm sure that some-body had to be monitoring this, you know, listening to it, but it was never stopped and no action was ever taken.

On occasions we were on the road. I don't know the name of the highway. As I said, I was a Pfc, and nobody ever told me much. It was between two LZs—LZ Baldy and LZ Ross. It was a fairly secure area. I don't think we ever received any fire. As I said, we were with a company of maybe 75 of us taking a break along the road. A Vietnamese civilian, wife and child, were riding down the road on a motorcycle, small motorcycle. Vietnamese were very ingenious and this guy had probably most of his possessions packed on the back of his motorcycle. We were sitting with this guy; I don't remember his name or rank. He had a scout dog with him. As the motorcycle was approaching us, he told the scout dog to get this guy. The dog jumped over the handlebars of the motorcycle, grabbed this guy off, had him by the leg, and was really doing a job on the guy's leg. This caused the motor-cycle to crash by the side of the road; the woman went one way, the baby went the other. All the possessions were all over the place. When we got to the guy, the dog trainer took the dog away from the guy. We went through his pockets. He had an ID card and a pass. As it turned out, he worked at either LZ Ross or LZ Baldy and had a pass signed by some military personnel. His motorcycle was wrecked. His wife had to push it down the road. He followed, limping, because he had blood pouring out of his leg, carrying most of his posses-sions and his young child. No action was ever taken against this guy. This was amusement, I suppose. There were at least 75 people watched this—four officers and I don't know how many E-7s and E-6s. Nothing was done.

Sgt. Ed Murphy, Americal Division

At the time most of this happened, our platoon leader was a Mormon minister. He's dead now so he can't really be found out and questioned. But when he got there, he was a pretty, well, high-character man because he was the minister.

47

By the time he got killed he was condoning everything that
was going on because it was a part of policy. Nobody told
you that it's wrong. This hell changed him around. And he
would condone rapes. Not that he would do them, but he
would just turn his head to them because who was he in a
mass military policy.

Lt. Jon Floyd, 1st Marine Division

I was a pilot with the Marine Corps and I served in Vietnam in 1968. I flew missions over both the North and the
South. I was discharged in December of 1969.

I was based with Marine Attack Squadron 533 in Chu
Lai. Most of our missions consisted of close air support,
which amounts to blowing the tops off of hills or something
for helicopters to land, and what is called a TPQ Mission,
which is a radar set. This guides the aircraft in at a high altitude, usually about 20,000 feet; they'll give us an air speed to
fly, an altitude, and heading control, and we'll reach a point
their gear tells them to tell us, and we release the bombs.
Sometimes we were told what our target was; the targets
might be a suspected enemy truck park, or a suspected
supply depot, or sniper fire. Normally we'd go up in either
single or section aircraft, two aircraft. We carried normally a
load of 28 five-hundred-pound bombs per aircraft, and it isn't
uncommon—it was a kind of standard joke—about releasing
56 five-hundred-pound bombs on a suspected sniper. The
TPQ bombing is a SEATO-level bombing, which is directly
condemned by the Nuremberg Principles after Dresden, in
World War II, was wiped out because no significant military
targets were there.

We also flew into North Vietnam. I was flying an A6A
Intruder aircraft, and this is a radar strike aircraft. We'd fly in
at a low level at night. They had stopped bombing Hanoi area
about two months after I arrived there. This type of mission
up into the Hanoi-Haiphong area, called Route Pack Six, was
called a "rolling thunder." Primarily what we did, while I was
there, was basically going in at night, low level, popping up to

48

about twelve hundred feet, acquiring a target on radar, and through the information from our various systems, it went into a computer; I pulled a commit switch and the computer dropped the bombs. We went back out low level. This was always done at night. I didn't get any rolling thunders while I was there, I'm not too unhappy to say.

Our bombing of the North mainly consisted of between the 17th and 18th parallels. This is where the Air Force and Marine Corps area was allotted when the bombing halt was called above the 20th parallel. The Navy had between the 18th and 19th parallels. Our primary objective was to pick up moving targets, such as trucks or barges—any convoys carrying supplies, etc. We also had secondary targets, which were normally called a truck park or a gun emplacement or ferry positions across the river, which we would drop our bombs on if we didn't pick up any moving targets. These were the same targets that we had for months and months, and they'd be bombed many times over each night.

Basically the type of weapons we used there were five-hundred-pound bombs, and two-thousand-pound bombs with what we called "daisy-cutters," which was about a yard-long fuse, to make sure that the bomb doesn't go ahead and penetrate the ground when it explodes but it stays above ground so the frag pattern will be large enough. We also used CBUs (cluster bomblet units), which are classified a secret I believe, which amount to a canister which releases a number of small bomblets which are anti-personnel. Also, we mined the rivers and roads with five-hundred-pound bombs which were set to go off normally in the 24-hour period following to catch trucks and barges coming along at later times.

Anywhere in North Vietnam basically is a free drop zone. There were no forbidden targets. If you didn't find any particular targets that you wanted to hit, then normally you'd go ahead and just drop your bombs wherever you wanted to. They had zones off in the water where you could go and jettison your bombs, but this was very seldom ever used. Many times, I know, a lot of pilots I've talked to said they would drop their bombs on the city of Dong Hoi, which is the main city between the 17th and 18th parallels there on the coast.

49

We had gotten information that the North Vietnamese had told us that they had a prisoner of war camp in Dong Hoi. It was always blacked out, but no one seemed to believe this and they'd go ahead and dump their bombs on the city there.

This war from the pilot's standpoint is a very impersonal war. You go over there and whether or not you believe the goals that the Government prescribes for us to fight for or whatever, most of the pilots just go along and figure, well, it's a job. And that's the way we all looked at it. You fly. You see flak at night. That's about as close to war as we get. Sometimes you get shot down, but you don't see any of the explosions. You can look back and see 'em, but you don't see any of the blood or any of the flesh. It's a very clean and impersonal war. You go out, fly your mission, you come back to your air-conditioned hootch and drink beer or whatever. You're not in contact with it. You don't realize at the time, I don't think, what you're doing. It dawned on me, I think, when we got reports of 13-year-old NVA soldiers coming across and being captured; that most probably they had young girls driving most of these trucks that we were destroying up north. And as far as the damage reports that were put out by the pilots, it was a kind of a standard joke. Especially when you knew which pilots would not particularly do a good job and every bomb they saw exploding, they'd come back and report secondaries. It was just a standard joke.

Sgt. Michael Hunter, 1st Air Cavalry Division and 1st Infantry Division

I am 24. I served in Vietnam two tours, the first tour was from the 1st Air Cav, Bravo Company 5th / 7th Air Cav; and the second tour was the 1st Infantry division, I Company, 75th Rangers, Lurps [LRRP], about 40 miles west of Saigon.

The first thing I want to bring to you is that I arrived in Vietnam during the Tet Offensive and Bravo Company, 5 / 7 was already outside of Hue. I flew out, and the second day that I was in the field, we came across a boy—he couldn't have been any older than 14—his arm was half, I'd say, 90

50

percent blown off. It was hanging by the skin, I mean it was hanging up to here. I requested—as a matter of fact, I didn't request, I demanded—from the medical NCO that we had there that something be done about him or else he'd die. He was so far gone, as far as deterioration, that he was stinking. You couldn't stand too near his body. The NCO said, "No, I don't want to waste my medical gear. It's no use now wasting our medical gear, because if we make contact we're going to need it. We don't have that readily available Medivac or the ships to supply us medical aid." I told my CO and he said, "Well, we don't have the time to stop and help him. He's going to die anyhow. We've got to move on because we got a mission to perform." That was the first incident.

Later, in between Hue Phu Bai and Camp Evans, which is also in the I Corps area, we came across and had an awful lot of fire fights with mainly the NVA. After the fire fight was over and the NVA were laying on the trail, we would approach the bodies, we'd shoot again to make sure that they were dead and then we'd carve—and I would say *we*, meaning myself also—carve Cav patches into his chest. And after that, if that wasn't sufficient (and this was done quite a few times), the heads of the bodies were cut off and they were placed on stakes, jammed down on stakes, and were placed in the middle of the trails and a Cav patch was hammered into the top of his head, with Bravo Company's "B" written right on the patch. Now this hasn't happened just once or twice, it happened five or six times. It didn't happen just in Hue Phu Bai, it happened around the Tay Ninh Province also, when the 1st Cav moved north or south.

We also dug up bodies, bodies that had been dead, gone for about three or four weeks, when we weren't making that much contact, and we would take the skulls and do the exact same thing—put them on the stakes on the trail, put another Cav patch on it, plus we would use them for body counts, repeated body counts. And what I'm saying, so no one will just misquote me, is that the body count given to the American public is extremely exaggerated. Every bunch of hootches that we came across (and I may say we didn't take activity around the roads unless we were resting) of huts numbering from six to twelve and on up, whether they were occupied or unoccupied, were burned. And if we didn't have the grenades or satchel charges to destroy the sanctuary holes for the Vietnamese, then we would tear them apart by hand. This was a standing order for Bravo Company 5 / 7, and it was standing order for 5 / 7 alone.

As far as CS gas, we always used CS. CS is the most powerful gas that can be used that will not kill you. It can create bodily harm if you're close—extremely bad burns. My CO of Bravo Company 5 / 7 gave an order, or I should say, gave permission to all the senior NCOs, the officers, and the enlisted men who were on guard on the outposts, to use CS on the civilian population who were congregating around the fences or the wires. Now this particular area was a rest area no more than 50 feet from a village directly on a road, and directly between a road and a bridge. The Vietnamese farms or their property lay on the other side of the bridge. They had to go past this bridge to get there. Smoke was constantly thrown outside the fence area at people walking by, and when the kids, and I do mean kids—four years old, ranging up to sixteen years old—came around the fence to sell GIs cigarettes, or candy, or beg for food, they were CS'd. And what I mean is they were gassed. This didn't happen just once, it happened constantly, the whole time we were there and when we were in base camp also. And when we didn't use CS out of the grenade we used CS out of the canister round of the M-79, which, if you're hit by it, you can be killed.

We were in a free fire zone just outside of Camp Evans and an old man, age 68 (I must say we could not tell that he was 68 at the time) was approximately 100 meters away from us cutting pineapple. It was very visible that he was cutting pineapple, and that he did not have a weapon. What he had was a machete. Machetes are carried in Vietnam by almost every civilian that works in the field and by the children. I was ordered by the senior NCO that was backing me up at the time, right behind me, to open fire. I opened fire and killed the man that was 68 years old. We found identification on his body stating that he was not a VC, not a Viet

52

Cong, not an NVA. He was a civilian and he did live in the nearby village, which was no more (and this was a free fire zone, I may add) than 1200 meters away. That was his farm-land that he was cutting down—the crops on the farmland. It was reported to the battalion that this was a body count. He had a weapon, the weapon being the machete. Suspected VC.

I served with I Company, 75th Rangers—excuse me, H Company, with the 1st Air Cav, and as you know, we do not have permission to cross the Laotian border. Up around A Shau Valley, which you might have heard of, or might not have, we crossed twice. When I say we, I say the teams that I was with; and we located enemy positions—how large the enemy was, its capability, and so on. That is not the thing. The fact is, we crossed a border line illegally. And you haven't heard anything about that yet.

As far as a date, as far as crossing the Laotian border, that took place in March 1968, twice. That was just prior to the A Shau Valley incident involving the 1st Air Cav. I, also, served with the 75th Rangers, I Company, attached to the 1st Infantry Division, just outside of Saigon. Prior to my getting there, in March, April, May, and June of '69, one helicopter of Lurps was sent across the Cambodian border-line, and I may add this was also illegal because we had no right in sending troops over there. The chopper was lost. It was hit by a B-40 rocket round and exploded in midair. We lost seven Lurps and four crewmen. Another time, another team was sent across the borderline, dropped off just short of it, walked across, and was never heard from again. To this day they are missing in action, presumably killed in Vietnam.

Now, as far as atrocities, my company, Bravo Company, 5th of the 7th, when we were outside of Hue shortly after the Tet Offensive, went into a village (and this happened re-peatedly afterwards) and searched for enemy activity. We encountered a large amount of civilian population. The civilian population was brought out to one end of the village, and the women, who were guarded by a squad and a squad leader at that time, were separated. I might say the young women were separated from their children and the older women and the older men, the elderly men. They were told

53

at gunpoint that if they did not submit to the sexual desires of any GI who was there guarding them, they would be shot for running away. And this was put in the language as best possible for people that cannot speak Vietnamese, and they got the point across because three women submitted to the raping of the GIs. I think that pretty well does it.

Question from audience: Mike, back to the body count. Were the body counts just enemy or were they men, women, and children? You said they were grossly exaggerated. Does that include the men, women, and children?

Hunter: A body count is a body count. I mean, that's exactly what it says. When the battalion commander calls up and says he wants a body count, if there are men, women, and children laying out there, he gets a body count of that many people. And usually we'd count about five bodies and it gets back there and it's about 25 or 15 bodies.

Panelist: I'd like to add something to that. I know on numerous occasions when we would receive contact in the field, we would call in support—artillery, gun ships (by that I mean helicopters), and if necessary, jet fighters. Now, every time someone is killed, there is kind of a dispute over who got him. So the Air Force claims one, the Artillery claims one, the Infantry claims one, and the gun ships claim one. So you've only got one body, but you've got four people claiming it.

Ah, I don't know. It was my distinct impression that during periods that I was over there, that we weren't winning the war.

Pvt. Jack Bronaugh, 1st Marine Division

I joined the Marine Corps about six months after getting out of high school. I was 18 years of age at the time. I enlisted for four years. I went to Vietnam in February of '68. I served with Echo Battery 2/13, attached to 2nd Battalion, 27th Marines.

Moderator: Which is the Fire Control Center?

54

Bronaugh: Right. It coordinates everything for the battalion artillery and troop movement and everything. I had some spare time this particular day so I left the compound and went to a bridge where people usually go and swim, and they had a detachment on this bridge, in total about two platoons of people. A 2nd lieutenant [was] in charge of the bridge and a gunnery sergeant that was staff NCO of the bridge. There were people from mortars platoon, weapons platoon, there was a tank, there were a couple of mules with 106 recoilless rifles, two snipers, and assorted machine gun crews.

This particular day I was going to go swimming and I was at this bridge and they had sent a patrol out from our battalion CP. They had gone north of the CP for about a half a mile or a mile. There was a few huts that comprised a small village north of the compound. The bridge got a radio call that they had supposedly received a sniper round from this village. So the lieutenant on the bridge told them to sweep the ville. They swept the ville and they called back that there was nothing found. There was nothing found; I mean, there were just people in the ville, and so the lieutenant told them to burn the ville.

From my position, which was about 150 to 200 yards away, and there was a tree line in the way, smoke started coming up over the tree line and about this time, I guess about three minutes after the smoke started showing, there was a lot of screaming and just chaos coming from the direction of the village and a lot of people started running out of the tree line. From where I was standing I saw maybe two or three male villagers and the rest were women and children—some of the children walking and some of them young enough to be carried, I would say under a year, maybe.

The last thing I heard as a command was the gunnery sergeant told them to open fire to keep them back. Their village was on fire and they were in panic; they didn't stop, so they just cut down the women and children with mortars, machine guns, tank; snipers were—

Moderator: There was a tank there also?

Bronaugh: Yes. Well, the tank, the 90 millimeter gun

wasn't used because, I mean, it was too close a range, but they used the 50 and the 30 off the tank and all the troops that were at the bridge with M-16s. The officer, a lieutenant, a few got close enough to where he used his 45. They used a few frag hand grenades.

Moderator: The fifty caliber. That was used specifically against the people?

Bronaugh: Yes . . . yes.

Moderator: Right. Just for general information, the 50-caliber machine gun is specifically forbidden to be used against people. It's an antivehicular weapon.

Bronaugh: Yes. It was used in automatic and single fire, against human beings.

S/Sgt. Franklin Shepard, 9th Infantry Division

I'm 23, from Plymouth, Michigan. I was a student before I entered the service. I'm a free spirit now. I was in the 5th Battalion, 60th Infantry, in the Headquarters Division, in the Personnel Department. Served in Vietnam from March of '68 to August of '69.

In our particular unit, we had this badge known as the Sat Cong badge. This badge, translated into English, means "Kill Cong." This represents one Viet Cong—or civilian, whatever it may be, because there's really no way of telling. It represents one life. These badges were given when someone could prove that he had killed a Viet Cong, or Vietnamese. There are many ways of doing this. One is to have somebody verify that you did in fact see him kill a Vietnamese. Another way is—and this is a common way—to cut off the ear of the dead Vietnamese and bring it in. You could exchange it for one of these badges. The badges were created on a battalion level; I have the order here that created this badge, and the sick individual that signed it.

Moderator: I tell you, Frank, on the "sick individual" let's just say "a captain in the infantry."

Shepard: All right. This is a disposition form. It's an official Army form dated 28 June '69. It reads as follows:

56

"Any member of this battalion who personally kills a Viet Cong will be presented a Sat Cong badge—Kill Viet Cong—for his gallant accomplishment. The Sat Cong badge will only be given to those individuals who have accomplished the above-mentioned feat. There will be no honorary presentations. Furthermore, only personnel who have personally killed a Viet Cong may wear the Sat Cong badge. Company Commanders will draw Sat Cong badges from the Executive Officer, and will maintain all control."

And also, explaining more about the badge. This is what is known as a Chieu Hoi leaflet. On one side, it's in Vietnamese; on the other side it's translated into English. This is used for two purposes: It's to build up the morale of the soldier, make him want to kill, and it's also to scare the hell out of the Viet Cong. It's entitled, *Viet Cong, N.V.A. Beware.* It says: "You are now located in the Area of Operations of the Cong-Killer 5th Battalion, 60th Infantry. Each member of this elite American unit is a trained killer, dedicated to the annihilation of every VC, NVA. The proof of this dedication is the Cong badge he proudly wears proclaiming he has personally killed a VC-NVA. We don't rest; we will hunt you with our helicopters, track you down with our radar, search above and below the water with boats, bombard you with artillery and air strikes. There are no havens here. You are not safe nor are you welcome here. Rally to the government of Vietnam now, or face the fact that you will soon join your ancestors. Signed, Cong-Killer 5th Battalion, 60th Infantry."

Moderator: That's sort of interesting, the "you are not safe nor are you welcome here"—this was in Vietnam, was it not?

Shepard: Yes, it's their country.

Moderator: Okay Frank, in talking about this, how do we know that these people were VC-NVA, rather than normal peasants?

Shepard: There's no possible way, really, to tell. As for myself, I never witnessed anyone cutting off an ear, for example, and bringing it in; I don't know that these were Viet Cong. It just seems that if you have something like this

57

you're going to get instances where people take civilians to get one of these badges. This was considered quite an honor, in fact, to have one of these badges. It was, it now seems rather sick, but over there it was the accepted thing that you were a real man if you had one. Some of them put oak-leaf clusters on the bottom if they killed more than one. Like I say, it's sick.

Moderator: Frank, the bottom line reads, "rally to the government of Vietnam now." Was this used as a Chieu Hoi pass, and if it was, or if it wasn't, were other Chieu Hoi passes accepted by your unit?

Shepard: No, there were the standard Chieu Hoi passes that are issued to all units; this was not considered a Chieu Hoi leaflet; this was more or less a threat. Now, if you were a civilian, imagine reading this in your village. This was dropped over populated areas. You can imagine reading this in your area. You'd be in fear for your life; afraid someone would take your ear and get one of these badges. If you collected so many badges, if you killed so many, you would get an R & R, or a pass. Get to go to Saigon, something like that. It was just part of the way to build up the body count.

Moderator: Okay, Frank, what was the purpose of these Sat Cong badges? For what were they designed—to up the morale, to up the body count, or what?

Shepard: Yes, up the body count, up the morale, make the men want to kill. As it said in the leaflet, it was, you know, "trained killers." The unit is full of trained killers.

Moderator: Another interesting thing that was brought out, these badges were made up at the local Vietnamese laundry.

Shepard: Cost the taxpayers 11 cents apiece.

Moderator: 11 cents apiece!

Shepard: All it is really, if you can't see it that well, it's just a cloth; it's regular O D, really, and it had the letters "Sat Cong" labeled on it, in hand, you know, or in a sewing machine. It's covered with plastic, and the ring at the top is to hang it over your button. They wear these to the field. Covered with plastic so the rain and the mud won't get at it. And people can see that you're a killer.

Moderator: Okay, do you have any evidence for the press that this actually did take place, other than your saying so?

Shepard: Yes, I do. I have two letters from the Defense Department admitting that the Sat Cong badge was initiated in my unit. They say the practice was discontinued after this letter was written. As I say, they do admit that it did happen. There's no question in their mind that it did happen. They pretend that they don't know the purpose for it, but as I say, I have the orders that were issued. I know the purpose for it, and everybody that was there knows the purpose for it. They say they can't do anything about this; they couldn't prosecute any individual, as they indicated they would if they could, because the commanding officer and the brigade commander were killed in a helicopter crash. Well, that's kind of funny. In the Calley case they say that they can't prosecute the higher officers because it's an individual thing, and there they turn it around. It's another inconsistency.

Moderator: If they wish to take action, then somebody has signed their name to this, and there is a live personnel.

Shepard: Yes, I believe he's responsible for it. I think he was taught in the Army that the reward system is a good system, and you should be given something to spur your men on to kill, and want to kill. I think this just came out of his own mind; I think it's sort of an isolated instance. But it is, of course, part of our general policy.

Patrick Ostrenga, 25th Infantry Division

I am currently a student at the University of Wisconsin in Madison. I was a medic with the 25th Division, Second Battalion, Twelfth Infantry, and attached to D-Company. My unit operated around Dau Tieng, which is about forty miles north of Saigon. I was working as a medic in Vietnam and there are quite a few things I can talk about. Well, one of the things I saw was one Vietnamese civilian, a pretty old man, was riding down a road with a bicycle. The lieutenant that was with us took out his M-16 and aimed it at the guy and

59

shot one round and, well, killed the guy. We went up to the guy, and he had a South Vietnamese ID card. Common practice in my unit was, if you killed a civilian with an ID card, you take his ID card and tear it up. The lieutenant's comment on this was, "Well, I guess I'm still a pretty good shot."

We took some prisoners one time, and one of them was wounded. The guy had a pretty big gash in his arm, some frag from some artillery. I went up to treat him, and as I was putting on the bandage, the guy was pulled away from me and the commanding officer, a captain, told me not to waste anything on the gooks except bullets. And, there were also some civilians that were wounded another time from some of our own artillery fire. I tried to treat some of them but I was told not to waste anything on them because they're not worth anything; they're just gooks. It's a very racist war.

WO Russel Kogut, 155th Assault Helicopter Company

I'm 22, I'm from Flint, Michigan. I was a Warrant Officer Helicopter Pilot with 155th Assault Helicopter Company in Ban Me Thuot. I will testify on illegal operations in Cambodia, on the destruction of livestock in free fire zones, burning of villages, forced evacuation of villages, and attitudes of Americans towards Vietnamese.

In July of '68 I worked with the Special Forces unit, B-50, out of Ban Me Thuot. Their main support were these Air Force helicopters here, the UH-IF, and you'll notice there are no markings on the aircraft. We were just being used as back-up because they were running more missions than they had aircraft for. And we supported them like this, on and off, for the whole year I was there and it continued after I was there. Our company took over a good deal more of this mission, as I was told by a friend of mine who came back.

We worked out of a base camp at Duc Lop down on the border. We put recon teams in consisting of two or three Americans and two or three hired—well, I can't swear that they were hired, but they were Cambodes or Montagnards, sympathetic with the U.S.—either for money or other rea-

60

sons, and we put these teams in. We went anywhere from one to three miles inside of Cambodia and, in the briefing that we received, they told us that their mission over there was to gather information on a known NVA unit that operated out of that area. The NVA had a base camp there of approximately 15,000 of them by the estimates gathered from these reports, from these spies that we took in. These missions were secret. The president had knowledge of these. I am informed that a copy of what goes on, goes to him. I can't verify that so I shouldn't say it, I guess. But, these missions continued up until the time of our going into Cambodia on the legitimate side and now they're no big thing.

Other testimony I have would be corroboration of these mad minutes. These things took place in our compound. They were quite common. Also, evacuation of villages. On occasion in Da Lat, a village southwest of Da Lat, we evacuated all the inhabitants and the ARVNs went through afterward and burned the whole village. The livestock that they didn't kill, they stole and brought back for themselves. I was on a similar type operation at Tuy An on the coast. A whole peninsula on the coast was said to be uninhabited and we went out there on these little search and destroy things. On one occasion they found a woman. We took her prisoner and she had a whole basement full of rice. They destroyed the house and I believe they destroyed all the houses in the village.

On one of these operations, as we were leaving the pickup zone, which is where we operated out of, somebody gave the okay for all the crew members to load rocks aboard the helicopter. Apparently the province chief, who is like God in these areas, said that it was okay for the gunners and crew chiefs to play bombardier by dropping rocks in the bay. He said anywhere over in this one part of the bay was okay to drop rocks. We took off to go pick up the troops. On the way we passed over this place, and all the crew members were throwing these rocks out. One sampan I know of was hit and sunk. There were two people in it. They swam to shore and another old man was hit by an ARVN captain. He threw the rock out and hit this old man right in the chest and at that

61

speed there's little doubt of what happened to him. The ARVNs burned the villages wherever they found rice because these missions were strictly one-day things and they didn't have time to haul rice out or investigate. The province chief decided where everybody was going to live, so if they didn't live where he wanted, they took the risk of having their houses burned.

Free fire zones are all over the place, wherever somebody decides to have one. We had one where we regularly tested our gun ships after they came out of maintenance. We took them out there, they would check them out, and anything in there was a free target. On one occasion I was flying north near a village called Ban Dong on a sniffer mission. For anybody not familiar with it, this is a device in a helicopter which detects ammonia scent emitted by humans. It's also emitted by monkeys. When they got a high enough count, they would bomb it, and either get monkeys or VC by their book. On this particular mission the gunships had to turn back early because they were low on fuel, and there was just myself with a sniffer and the commanding patrol ship, which was a ways above me with a map. I saw an elephant and made mention of the fact. The captain who was in charge of the overall mission told me to go back and look and see what was going on. I went back. There were four adults and a calf. I circled them several times. There was no village in the vicinity, so they were not friendly elephants, and there were no (this was by the captain's definition) there were no marks on the elephants or packs or any signs of any people around, so I assumed they were wild. The captain assumed they were enemy and told me to have 'em destroyed. So I had my gunners shoot 'em. And this is the price an animal pays for being wild in Vietnam. The same thing goes for water buffalo. Several times I've seen water buffalo shot for sport. If they were on a certain side of a ridge or on the other side of a river, they were considered fair game.

Lt. Sam Bunge, 101st Airborne Division

I served in Vietnam for one year between July of '68 and June of '69. During that time I had a succession of jobs. First I was a rifle platoon leader, a grunt, for three or four months. Then I was a battalion staff officer, and my final five months in country I was in charge of the brigade security platoon. My unit operated in the vicinity of Cu Chi, which is between Saigon and Cambodia. Then we were transferred up to I Corps and operations were conducted west of Phu Bai in the mountains.

The incidents I have to recount are just in random order. Camp Evans, which is the next base camp up the country from Sally, also had trash dumps outside the wire. This was standard procedure all over Vietnam because I heard other people complaining about the practice. Civilians would get into our trash dump, too, and we routinely used CS to disperse the civilians. They kept coming back, of course. I observed many instances of H & I (harassing and interdicting fire), which is artillery fire pooped out at irregular intervals at indiscriminate targets around the fire base just with the idea of keeping the enemy off guard in case he's coming up.

When I first took over my platoon, we were on a sweep operation and we received a couple of rounds of sniper fire from a village in an area that we knew had a lot of VC. The civilians weren't terribly sympathetic to them or to us. So we went over to the village to check it out, to look for weapons, to see what was in there. We'd been there several times before and after we'd reached the center of the hamlet (it wasn't a very big place), I noticed that a couple of haystacks were on fire in an area that we'd already come through. I asked the squad leader of the 3rd squad back there why that was and he said, "Well, that's SOP." And I said, "No, it's not." He said, "Well, the other lieutenant (referring to my predecessor) said that if we ever get sniper fire from a village we were supposed to burn it down." So after we got the village secure, I called all the squad leaders together and changed the policy. The point here is, that in a war like Vietnam where small unit commanders have such autonomy (lieutenants and captains to a large degree run the show), an individual can make a big difference. If a man wants to burn villages, he can do it.

Quite a bit later, as I said, when I had the security platoon up north, we had a problem with civilians in the trash dump. One day we picked up about a dozen kids; they were all boys ranging in age from twelve down to about six. I got an order from the brigade commander through headquarters company commander to hold the kids in the POW cage for 48 hours without food or water to teach them a lesson. I didn't want to do this. I argued a little bit and I said, "You know, prisoners are the responsibility of the MPs. Why don't you give it to them?" We had an MP platoon stationed at Camp Evans, and finally he admitted that the MPs wouldn't do it because they realized it was illegal too.

So I went away, thought about it for a while, then went back to my company commander, and said, "Sir, I can't do this. It's illegal. How about backing me up? We'll go tell the colonel that we can't do it." And he says, "No, I won't." So I went looking for the brigade executive officer to try to get his backing and I couldn't find him. Finally I decided what I should do. They probably wouldn't check on me, so I just disobeyed the order without telling anybody. When I got up to the cage to tell the platoon to feed 'em, but to be discreet about it, the kids were already eating. So, the problem was circumvented. The kids weren't actually kept 48 hours. We let 'em go after about 36. They spent the night there. The place we kept them in was actually a decent place; it was a plywood building reinforced with wire so they couldn't get out. So, the mistreatment of prisoners was not done, but it was intended to be done.

Several times while flying back and forth between the mountains and Camp Evans, I observed an operation on the ground called "Rome Plowing," which I don't think has come out before. A Rome Plow is a very large tractor; the driver sits inside a heavy reinforced cage, and if you can imagine a giant snowplow on the front, it's very similar to clearing snow except that it clears ground. As it drives along, it uproots and pushes aside all vegetation so what you're left with is an area that looks like a bulldozed area. A Rome Plow is good because it can push over trees; it can do a large area in a very short time. This was being used to clear a patch about 500 to 1000 meters wide down the base of the mountains so that it would be easy for air observers to detect anybody coming in and out of the mountains. They wouldn't be hidden by the foliage. A mechanical sort of defoliation rather than the chemical sort. I used, several times, chemical Agent Orange around the perimeter of Camp Evans in an effort to clear the underbrush. They gave us about ten 55-gallon barrels of it, and we sprayed the stuff all around. There were two villages adjacent to the area and we didn't spray these villages intentionally, of course, but we got pretty close.

When I was a grunt platoon leader, we were moving across a rice paddy and were reconning by fire in a tree line on the other side. When we got there, there was a village right there, a lady came out and told us that her mother had been wounded by a frag from one of our M-79 rounds. So I told the medic to patch her up and stopped the platoon to provide him with security. It took about fifteen minutes to dress her wound and give her some antibiotic. The whole time the company commander was hassling me about why didn't I just leave her alone and hurry and catch up with the rest of the company. He didn't want me to stay back there.

Another time, the company was together and we were moving in on an area to reinforce another company that was in contact. We were back in the staging area waiting for the battalion CO to tell us exactly where to go. I happened to be up talking to the CO and his headquarters group spotted a farmer plowing, or doing something, with a buffalo in his fields—maybe 500 meters away—a considerable distance. Some of the EM in the headquarters section got the idea that they'd get some target practice on this individual. My memory is not clear whether the CO participated—I know he actively participated as a spectator and sort of encouraged this, but I can't tell you whether he pulled any triggers himself or not. But they fired on this man. The farmer had been doing nothing hostile, just minding his own business, just walking across the dyke or something. But they fired on him, single shot with an M-60 machine gun, and they were obviously doing it just for sport because they did it shoulder fire, which is extremely inaccurate. If they'd felt it had a military necessity, they would've put the gun down on a bipod and done it accurately. And when they didn't hit the fellow, and evidently he didn't notice because he kept going, they set up the 81 Mike-Mike mortar and pooped out a few high explosive rounds at him. He went down and my suspicion is that he went down just to get us to leave him alone, but we never did go and check.

At one point we were going into a village which we had reason to believe had a lot of weapons in it. As a matter of fact, we did find a few weapons. But we didn't find nearly as many as we expected. So we found a grave, an old grave, obviously an old grave, an old tombstone in the red-pitted rock that they make tombstones out of, and the CO said, "Gee, there might be something buried in that grave because the VC sometimes do that. So let's dig down a little bit." We dug down about two feet and obviously the ground hadn't been disturbed for years because it was the same color and the same density that the ground always was. But something had caught the CO's imagination, so he made us keep going and eventually we got down to the casket. He told us to break it open, so we broke it open. There was nothing inside. Evidently, his whole motivation for disinterring this grave and disturbing the corpse was simple morbid curiosity.

When I was back with the brigade again, my platoon was given the assignment one month to implant a series of six sensor fields out in the mountains in an uninhabited area. The area was literally uninhabited. I flew over the area many times and there were no traces of anybody ever having lived there. These are electronic devices that you bury in the ground to detect through various means. One means is seismic, one is infrared, and another is magnetic. If anybody passes near them, they send out a signal. A man on the fire base reads the signal and tells the fire direction control center. They fire artillery on the target and what's bad about it is they don't know who it is they're firing on. It's done without any positive identification. You just pick up the impression of somebody out there, check with the infantry

TOC to make sure it's nobody friendly, assume it's enemy, and fire 'em up. That's the way these things are intended to be used.

SP/4 Timon Hagelin, 1st Logistics Command

I'm from Philadelphia. I was in the Graves Registration Platoon attached to 223rd Field Service Company, 1st Logistics Division.

I was at Dak To at two different times. The first time was about a month after I got in the country. I came in country with the MOS of shoe repairman. And when I got to my field service unit they said that I had a choice of baking bread or picking up dead bodies. So I told them that I wanted to go to the field to see what was happening. They sent me up there. While I was on the base taking care of KIAs [killed in action] as they came through, I made friends with people in my company that I considered basically nice people. We used to get together at night and talk. I went down to a certain place where they all were and as I approached it, I heard a scream. Someone was obviously very scared. As I got down to the door, I called one of my friends. He punched this chick on the side of the head. The girl was, you know, Vietnamese people are a lot smaller than American people. It doesn't take that much to hurt one of those people, you know. They gave her a couple good shots and the girl finally started yelling "Me do, me do, me do" and about seven of them ripped her off. I know the guys, and I know basically they're not really bad people, you know. I just couldn't figure out what was going on to make the people like this do it. It was just part of the everyday routine, you know.

And the second time I was on Dak To we were getting KIAs in from that battle of Ben Het. One day we were at the mortuary, you know, the tent that we used to process KIAs. We saw a body laying out in the runstrip and we went and picked up the body. It was maybe like a hundred degrees out; the heat was beating down. The body was wrapped up in a poncho liner, which isn't too good for the preservation of the body. We brought it inside and it turned out to be a Montagnard. Now Americans don't handle any KIAs but their own. They can't give you one rule for why they don't, but they just don't want to be bothered. The Vietnamese or the Montagnards are just treated as animals. They know they're human beings but they really don't treat them that way. It's like they're a lesser thing; they're a lesser type human being. Anyway, it was a KIA from a straight force, a Mike force. That was Special Forces, you know. The Special Forces guy came in and he said, "I'll just put the body back on the runway because it's just a dead 'yard you know. Just leave him out there." This was the person that was supposedly helping these people out. And going out in the jungles with them—"it's just a dead 'yard, you know; like forget about him."

There was also an incident in Pleiku where the Special Forces E-5 from Pleiku did 'em a favor. He put a Montagnard body in one of our reefers. We had two or three reefers turned on for American KAIs and then we had spare reefers that we didn't always use—refrigeration to keep the KIAs. The 'yard was in there for about five days. The guy that put him in there forgot that he was in there and the body was just laying inside this reefer for five days. That's like putting it in an oven. And finally, two of my friends were walking through the mortuary, and they smelled something. When they opened it up, the guy was really very . . . like, you know, he was really . . . after five days inside that thing. And the action taken against the E-5 that did it was Article 15—you know, they called him stupid. They took some of his money away from him for destroying a Montagnard body.

Pfc. Charles Leffler, 9th Marine Amphibious Brigade

I live in Detroit and I was formerly with Battalion 226, Golf Company, the 9th Marine Amphibious Brigade in Vietnam. I was in Vietnam from September 1968 to September 1969.

In January 1969 we were on a sweep. We were on line

68

through a series of rice paddies and villages in Quang Nam province, which is just southwest of Da Nang. We'd received a battalion order at that time and the order stated that this order would take effect from that day forward until a rescinding order would come through. It never came through in the next eight months, until after I returned, so the battalion order was always in effect. If while sweeping on line and passing by friendly villages, which we did, you received one round of any sort from a friendly village, the entire battalion was to turn on line and level that village. The exact wording was to kill every man, woman, child, dog, and cat in the village. This was *one* round from any known friendly village.

Cpl. William Hatton, 3rd Marine Division

I'm 23 and I was a high school student before I entered the Marine Corps in 1966. I spent 4 years in regular enlistment. I attained the rank of Corporal, as a Lance Corporal and Corporal both, during my tour. I was in Vietnam from October of 1968 to September of 1969. My outfit was Engineer Maintenance Platoon, FLSG Bravo, Dong Ha. At present, I'm the director of the Department of Planning Promotion for the village of Bagley, Minnesota.

When I arrived in Vietnam my MOS was a heavy equipment mechanic. Since there wasn't a real need for my billet to be filled as a mechanic, I was put in my secondary MOS, which was 8151, that of a security guard. Since I filled this billet so admirably, they kept me going on perimeter, which was in a sense a shit detail that they send people they don't like out on. Since I wasn't the most popular type of personality, there I went. Well, at any rate, my duty was to go out and serve as a perimeter guard on the Dong Ha ramp. This was an LCU ramp on the Quat River where Navy ships came up and they'd off-load supplies.

We took our truck outside the combat base every night at 5:30 to set up at the ramp for our night's duty. We used to drive by this row of hootches and a little three-year-old kid in a dirty grey shorts used to run out and scream, "You,

Marines, Number 10" and we'd always go back, "Oh fuck you, kid" and all this stuff. So one night the kid comes out and says "Marine, you Number 10" and throws a rock. So we figured we'd get him because this was a way of having fun. The next night before we went out we all stopped by COC, which is right by the ammo dump, picked up the biggest rocks we could get our hands on and piled them in the back of the truck. So when we left the combat base we just turned the corner and we saw a little kid, we were waiting for the kid—he ran out of the hootch—and he was going to scream "Marine, Number 10" and we didn't even let him get it out of his mouth. We just picked up all the rocks and smeared him. We just wiped him out. In fact, the force of the rocks was enough to knock over his little tin hootch as well. I can't say that the kid died, but if it would have been me, I would have died easily. The rocks, some of them, were easily as big as his head. It was looked upon as funny. We all laughed about it. And then we forgot about it.

It took me about a year to even to be able to recall the situation. I think it said something about the entire attitude of us over there. I never had a specific hatred for the Vietnamese, I just tended to ignore them. They didn't figure in any calculations as to being human. They either got in the way or they weren't there. And also, we had this habit, when we'd leave the combat base—I frequently traveled between Quang Tri and Dong Ha and contact teams, and we'd take C-ration crackers and put peanut butter on it and stick a trioxylene heat tab in the middle and put peanut butter around it and let the kids munch on it. Now they're always looking for "Chop, chop" and the effect more or less of trioxylene is to eat the membrane out of your throat and if swallowed, would probably eat holes through your stomach.

Another portion of the testimony that I would like to cover is that in March of '69 I was serving as security in a convoy, and this wasn't actually in line of duty; I was able to have a day off and I was going down to Quang Tri so I got on a truck belonging to 7 Motors. They were in convoy; they just gave me a ride at the gate and we got four miles south of the Dong Ha perimeter and there were a group of Vietnamese women and children who were gathered around at this little bridge outpost the ARVNs had as security on Highway 1 there. The truck was doing considerable speed and it was just sort of a spontaneous reaction, they said, "Let's get 'em. They want chop, chop, we'll give it to 'em;" picking up cases of C-rats, which weigh up to approximately thirty pounds, and threw them off into the women and the kids. You know, just flattened them out and knocked them back quite a few feet. There again, there was no way of determining whether or not they were actually dead but the injuries must have been serious.

The whole thing, like I mentioned with the garbage trucks—I never experienced shooting anybody off garbage trucks, but many times we put our boots in the faces of kids and women who'd crawl all over it. There used to be a game we played—we'd pour liquid garbage off the end of our truck to make 'em crawl for it. The mama-sans would come up with half-cut 50-gallon drums and they'd try to fill it up. They'd get pork chops and sloppy rice, and mystery meat or wop slop, or whatever we had for chow, and put it in there and we'd let 'em walk so far and then we'd tip it over, spill it on the ground, and watch them scrape the dirt in there. Anything to dehumanize them. I think the program went even farther. We used to have kids from the orphanage visit us aboard Dong Ha and have a party for them so that we could play games like holding sodas in the air and watch them grasp for it; patting them on the head and teaching them little tricks like how to beg for candy bars.

A further part of my testimony is like with mad minutes. As I traveled variously around northern I Corps, I used to go to a place called "Stud," which was later gloriously reclassified as Combat Base Vandegrift. This was due to the John Wayne syndrome, which is pretty prevalent in the Marine Corps. They just don't name anything a plain name; it has to have glorious connotations. I had gone over to visit some friends of mine at 3rd Shore Part and we went over to have a little party out there on the lines, and nobody gave me the word that we were going to have a mad minute. What happens with a mad minute is that everybody opens up, at least half the guys on each bunker and every sector of the line open up with four deuces—the guys in support—and they'll fire for two or three minutes. They call it mad minutes. This in effect kills anything. You don't know what's out there and neither do they. You just fire in the hope that you're going to get something. You cease fire and you wait for a reaction and there's usually none. It's more or less a waste of ammunition. This I witnessed about two or three times. Like I said, I was never assigned, as a guard, to do mad minutes, but I was witnessing it.

You know, if Vietnam is not violently painful then it's such a crashing bore that you can't stand it.

Sgt. Joe Bangert, 1st Marine Division

I'm a Philadelphia resident. I enlisted in the Marine Corps for four years in 1967. I went to Vietnam in 1968. My unit in Vietnam was Marine Observation Squadron 6 with the 1st Marine Air Wing, and my testimony will cover the slaughter of civilians, the skinning of a Vietnamese woman, the type of observing our squadron did in Vietnam, and the crucifixion of Vietnamese, either suspects or civilians.

The first day I got to Vietnam I landed in Da Nang Air Base. From Da Nang Air Base I took a plane to Dong Ha. I got off the plane and hitchhiked on Highway 1 to my unit. I was picked up by a truckload of grunt Marines with two company grade officers, 1st lieutenants. We were about 5 miles down the road where there were some Vietnamese children at the gateway of the village and they gave the old finger gesture at us. It was understandable that they picked this up from the GIs there. They stopped the truck—they didn't stop the truck, they slowed down a little bit, and it was just like response—the guys got up, including the lieutenants, and just blew all the kids away. There were about five or six kids blown away and then the truck just continued down the hill. That was my first day in Vietnam.

As far as the crucified bodies, they weren't actually crucified with nails, but they would find VCs or something (I never got the story on them) but, anyway, they were human beings, obviously dead, and they would take them and string them out on fences, on barbed wire fences, stripped, and sometimes they would take flesh wounds, take a knife and cut the body all over the place to make it bleed and look gory as a reminder to the people in the village.

Also in Quang Tri city I had a friend who was working with USAID and he was also with CIA. We used to get drunk together and he used to tell me about his different trips into Laos on Air America Airlines and things. One time he asked me would I like to accompany him to watch. He was an advisor with an ARVN group and Kit Carsons. He asked me if I would like to accompany him into a village that I was familiar with to see how they act. So I went with him and when we got there the ARVNs had control of the situation. They didn't find any enemy but they found a woman with bandages. So she was questioned by six ARVNs, and the way they questioned her, since she had bandages, they shot her. She was hit about 20 times. After she was questioned, and, of course, dead, this guy came over who was a former major—been in the service for twenty years—and he got hungry again and came back over working with USAID, Aid International Development. He went over there, ripped her clothes off, and took a knife and cut from her vagina almost all the way up, just about up to her breasts and pulled her organs out, completely out of her cavity, and threw them out. Then he stooped and knelt over and commenced to peel every bit of skin off her body and left her there as a sign for something or other; and that was those instances.

Moderator: Okay, there were American officers present when this happened or?

Bangert: There were two super secret, I know they were field grade officers, who were with MACV in Quang Tri province in the area. They knew about it.

I used to work with the pacification program in Vietnam and I traveled extensively through Quang Tri province. Specifically in the area of Quang Tri city and west, Trieu Phong District, I saw approximately during my tour 20 deformed infants under the age of one. It never made sense to me; I thought it was congenital or something, from venereal

73

disease, because they had flippers and things. I didn't understand what I saw until approximately six months ago I read a report that was put out by Stamford which talked about the thalidomide content within Agent Orange. And it was common knowledge that Agent Orange was sprayed in the area, and we used to see it about every three to four days where I was in Quang Tri province.

CWO Dennis Caldwell, 1st Aviation Brigade

I'm 24, from Ypsilanti, Michigan. I was a Warrant Officer flying gun ships from October '68 to October '69 in Vietnam. I flew for the 3/17th Air Cav, which was not part of the 1st Air Cav. It was part of the 1st Aviation Brigade. I was a helicopter Cobra gun ship pilot. I worked with another aircraft at all times; 90 percent of the time it was called a hunter-killer team. A hunter-killer team goes out and does reconnaissance on certain areas. The other aircraft that was with me was a small observation helicopter, normally OH6A Cayuse.

Every morning we'd go out and look at certain targets, certain coordinates that were given to us in the morning. We spent about two hours in the morning, plus or minus an hour, sometimes all day, looking at targets, and also just before sundown we would do this. During the day we were on call for any ground units that got into contact. I was told by the other pilots in the unit how to tell a VC from a civilian—if they were running, they were VC. If they were standing there, they were well-disciplined VC, and shoot 'em anyhow. They also told me that when we were flying over a village, or near a village, if people started to leave the village, civilians, it was a good sign that there were VC in the area, that they were expecting a fight.

It was a perfectly normal, standard operating procedure for my unit and many other units to recon by fire. It's done with a mini-gun, which fires (I can't remember exactly what it is) 3- or 4000 rounds a minute. It was done using CS grenades; it was done using 40-millimeter grenades; it was done using 2.75-inch rockets, with either 10- or 17-pound warheads of various combinations. As far as clearance to fire went, my first three months I never heard of the term "clearance to fire." If there was somebody that we thought might be VC by his actions, by running or hiding, he was a dead man.

Ninth Division were people that we supported mainly when I first got to Vietnam. We had pretty much our own show. We didn't have to ask anybody what to shoot. We didn't have to ask for clearance. After that we worked closer to Saigon. We worked probably within a 30- or 40-mile radius of Saigon in all directions, and we had extreme trouble receiving clearance to fire. An Air Force forward controller, who coordinates air strikes from jets, told me one time, "If you have trouble obtaining clearance to fire, just holler out that you're receiving fire, and we'll send jets in to bomb the hell out of the place, whether or not you actually receive fire, or whether or not there are any weapons in the area at all."

Free fire zones—I worked in many free fire zones. It's kind of hard to number them because almost every day, some place, we'd come in contact with a free fire zone. I've seen hootches burned down which were not proven to be military targets. I've seen hootches CS'd to drive people out. When the people were driven out, naturally running away (who wants to hang around and breathe the CS for an hour), they were killed.

I have seen a prisoner beaten. He was in a cold area; no fire was received from this area. This was to the northwest of Saigon, to the south of Cu Chi. I can't remember the exact location. We'd been called out to do a recon in this area. It's quite desolate. It was at least a couple of kilometers from any real village, any settlement. Along this canal line, this man was hiding. I do not know whether or not he was armed. But I know that there was no fire received in that area from any enemy soldiers. They flushed this guy out. They tied his hands behind his back. The water was approximately a foot deep in this rice paddy where they were working him over. I was watching from approximately 500 feet. He was kicked. He was beaten in many ways. Kneeling in this water, with his hands behind his back. I don't know if he was blindfolded or not. Being repeatedly knocked down into the water, set back upright, hit again, and knocked down.

Concerning 50-caliber machine guns, many, many times I have seen them mounted on the doors of Hueys, specifically to be used against ground troops. That's what you go up for is to kill ground troops. Go up in conjunction with firefly ships used at night, used at day, and this is fairly well known among us.

I have seen, several times, C-123 aircraft working to the west of Saigon. There's a large river that's to the west of Saigon, runs roughly north and south. I can't remember the name of it at the moment, but beyond this river there is absolutely nothing left. There were hundreds and hundreds of villages marked on the map that I had with me, all kinds of names on the map, but you get over that area and there's nothing there at all. It's all been wiped out long ago. Now the C-123's are going out to that area with defoliant, I don't know exactly what chemical it was. I've seen formations of six C-123's out there, low-level spraying, with Air Force jets providing cover for them. And I believe there was one time we were to be on stand-by for these people; in fact, I'm sure of it. There was one time we were to be on stand-by for these people in that general area in case they ran into any ground fire. I have seen a herd of water buffalo CS'd because nothing was going on, the pilot flying the LOACH [Light Observation Air Controller Helicopter] was getting bored and saw the water buffalo; he dropped one or two CS grenades on them and they stampeded. They crashed into a bunch of foliage next to the river and they went head over heels into the river, you know; it just completely drove them crazy. I don't know what happened to them after that. I don't know if water buffalo can swim or not. I never saw any swimming.

Pfc. Walter Hendrickson, 3rd Marine Division

I'm 22. I'm a resident of upstate New York. I'm unemployed now because of disability. I entered the Marine Corps shortly after working 6 months as a turret lathe operator. I was trained as an antitank personnel and when I reached Vietnam I was made a regular rifleman grunt.

I spent from November of 1968 to April of 1969 where I was wounded on an operation in Laos and I really don't remember what the operation's name was because we never were told. We just knew that we had landed right near the Laotian border and we had a sniper unit with us who worked right inside of Laos and all our LPs—our listening posts— which were at night and our observation posts in the day-time—all were in Laos, plus the fact that we did run patrols constantly through Laos. Also, before we started this opera-tion, we were Tet Offensive in the MACV compounds where we worked out of right around Mai Loc, which is in the Quang Tri province. And working around there the squad I was in, we run into an NVA observation post, it must have been, because they were all sitting around the fire and the point man and the man behind him, I'm quite sure they killed three of the five men and the other two were wounded. My team leader at the time was right up front there giving orders and one of the NVA threw his rifle down—he was wounded—and he was crying, "Chieu Hoi, Chieu Hoi" and my team leader just said, "Burn him" and he was shot to death. Then we were told to pull back and we were working with a 1st lieutenant, he was a tank commander, he was out with us because we were working with the tanks and he called the tanks up on line and they proceeded to shoot into these wounded NVA, beehive rounds and HE rounds, plus they were firing from their 30-caliber machine guns.

"Chieu Hoi" is a Vietnamese word for surrendering. In other words he'll "Chieu Hoi" if he doesn't want any more of fighting. Pretty near every grunt over there, I would say, knows the meaning of "Chieu Hoi," but the six months I spent over there before I was wounded, we never took a prisoner. I can remember one time in the village, we brought a person in for questioning and he was released the next day, but we never took any prisoners. We really never got an order to take prisoners and I think it was a general attitude of almost everybody over there not to take a prisoner. All the while I was over in Vietnam we were pretty much in a free fire zone, and if we saw anybody out there we didn't even attempt to take a prisoner; we just opened fire.

Lt. Mark Lenix, 9th Infantry Division

I'm 24 years of age. I was a lab technician before I went in the service. I was drafted. I was a 1st lieutenant, served with the 1st/11th Artillery attached to the 2nd/39th Infantry Battalion as a Forward Observer.

H & I was to sort of keep the VC off guard. You weren't sure what was there, but if they were, then of course you just drop artillery on top of them. When I was working with H & I fire, you'd put your arms out and the only clearance you'd have would be from battalion. You'd call them, give them a grid square, and they'd say, "Sure, there's nothing there. Go ahead and shoot." And then, of course, you'd send the order to the guns and the guns would shoot. Well, on one instance that I can remember, there was nobody there and we went ahead and shot. The next day a papa-san brought in his dead wife and wounded baby. There was nobody there.

In November '68, in an area called the Wagon Wheel, which is northwest of Saigon, while on a routine search and destroy mission, gun ships which were providing security and cover for us in case we had any contact, were circling overhead. Well, no contact was made, and the gun ships got bored. So they made a gun run on a hootch with mini-guns and rockets. When they left the area we found one dead baby, which was a young child, very young, in its mother's arms, and we found a baby girl about three years old, also dead. Because these people were bored; they were just sick of flying around doing nothing. When it was reported to battalion, the only reprimand was to put the two bodies on the body count board and just add them up with the rest of the dead people. There was no reprimand; there was nothing. We tried to call the gun ship off, but there was nothing you could do. He just made his run, dropped his ordinance, and left. And there they were, man. The mother was, of course, hysterical. How would you like it if someone came in and

78

shot your baby? And there was nothing we could do, man, I just watched it. And nothing happened. I have no idea what happened to the helicopter pilot, or to anyone in the gun ship. It was gone. Things like this happen, I'm sure, more than once, because if I saw it, I'm sure a lot of veterans who aren't here saw it.

And this is why we have to stop the war. Because not only are we killing our brothers in the armed forces, and brothers on the other side, but we're killing innocent people, man, innocent civilians, who are just standing by and happen to be at the place at that time, and for no other reason than that, wind up dead.

SP/4 Michael Misiaszek, 101st Airborne Division

I'm from Reading, Pennsylvania. I was with the 101st in the 1st Brigade, Support Element. We rigged up the choppers to fly supplies out to the troops and sometimes we'd go out and hand them out wherever they were. That was the last half. The first half, I was actually just a telephone answerer. I was in Vietnam from the first of December 1968 to the end of January 1970. This was at Camp Eagle and I was also down at Tam Ky after I got fired from my office job. My testimony concerns a whole bunch of things. Most of it's been heard before. I'd just like to elaborate on it for those who may not have been here before.

The first thing I'd like to talk about is the destruction of a cemetery. The entire northeast corner of the 101st base camp, Camp Eagle, southwest of Hue, is built on a Vietnamese cemetery. They didn't plow under any graves; they didn't have to. They just built the compound on top of it, which means that there are still graves between some of the buildings. Some of the buildings are on top of old graves which had been plowed under and are all misshapen. I'd like to talk about harassment fire. Where we were sleeping was pretty close to a battery of 8-inch howitzers. These are big guns, man. They go off and they shake the ground. I think the round is as long as this table, maybe. And there's a lot of high explosives in there. They fired these things indiscriminately. They woke us up, they shook the whole place, and several of us got really pissed off. We wanted to find out why they were doing this all the time. This was every night. We talked to a specialist up in the battery, and he said they had orders to fire no less than thirty rounds nightly at a strip west of Camp Eagle. This strip was supposedly a free fire zone. Anybody could have been walking in there, like even some of our own people from other units, but they didn't really seem to care. They just shot this thing up.

Another thing I'd like to talk about is the use of some chemical agents. On our perimeter we had CS gas, little canister with tear gas I guess, and what's known as Fugas. I don't know if anyone has brought this up. Fugas is a jelly-like substance. It's flammable, and they put it in barrels. What they do to it is they explode the barrel over an area and this flaming jelly-like substance lands on everything, if it's people or animals or whatever. And you can't get it off. It just burns, and you rub it and it sticks on. You just spread it all around. The only way to stop it is by suffocating it in mud or water. This was not around too often during the dry season, you know.

When we were at Tam Ky, we convoyed in August back to Camp Eagle. They put a whole bunch of guys on a truck and we had C-rations. We made a pretty good game out of throwing C-rations at civilians as hard as we could. Then we tried to see if we could maybe get them through the grass huts. Like we would throw them at a grass hut. It would go through and we'd wait and see if someone comes out yelling or something.

I'd also like to talk about mad minutes. This was mentioned before. Our mad minutes, for those of you who may not have heard it, were at the perimeter fence. Every once in a while at Camp Eagle, every two months or so, the order would just come down, "Okay guys, go to it." You got a mad minute. And everybody picks up a weapon with both hands, both feet, and they shoot. And they don't care what they shoot at, just as long as it's away from the base area. That's a lot of fun, too. All those sickies.

80

Major Jon Bjornson, 8th Field Hospital

I was formerly a major, U.S. Army Medical Corps. I have my DD-214 right here, which is an honorable discharge form. I was a psychiatry-neurology consultant in Vietnam through 1964-1965. I also functioned for five months as a Flight Surgeon in the Mekong Delta and was Deputy Surgeon, United States Support Command at the time.

We used a combination of gases there called CS, CN, and I think DM. These are a nauseant, a mucous irritant, and a tearing gas, a lacimating agent. I knew we used these because I saw them used. On Christmas day in 1964 we were attempting to recapture eight Americans somewhere in the area of Tay Ninh. We were attempting to recapture Americans who had been captured by the Vietnamese. They were going to blanket a large area near the Black Virgin Mountain where they thought these prisoners were. They mixed this gas on a soccer field which was adjacent to an airfield on one side and the hospital for Tay Ninh on the other side. They had large drums, they would mix them, and they would put them in a rocket pod of an armed helicopter. While there were mixing them, a helicopter landed improperly behind the area where they were mixing and a large cloud of gas settled over the entire city of Tay Ninh, including us. That included the hospital. Now these gases are said not to be lethal. Unfortunately they are lethal if you have pulmonary disease. If you happen to get nauseated and vomit when you've had abdominal surgery, it can be pretty serious. And if you happen to have an open wound with a nerve exposed, it will cause direct nerve damage. This whole hospital was covered with this gas which poured down over the area.

Sgt. Fred Nienke, 1st Marine Division

I joined the Marine Corps shortly after graduating from high school in 1966. I went to Vietnam and was assigned to Delta, 1st Battalion, 5th Marines.

I think every person who was in Vietnam who was in the

Infantry used CS, which is a gas; chemicals; Willie Peter—
that's White Phosphorus—and we used these sometimes to
clear bunkers and other times to destroy a hootch. We used
to think that was kicks; there would be people in a hootch or
something like this and we'd throw in a gas grenade and
they'd cough and then we'd leave.

And other times we used to use—we had mortar squads in
the infantry used to avoid going into a village or something if
we though it might be VC infested or something like this,
we'd send in Willie Peter mortars, 60 millimeters, and this
would burn up the hootches, that explode throwing white
phosphorus on different hootches in the village. Start the
hootches burning and also kill people. It's probably one of
the worst sights I've ever seen is a person that's been burned
by Willie Peter because it doesn't stop. It just burns all
completely through your body. The only way you can end
this burning is to cut off the air. It's very difficult.

SP/4 Allan Crouse, 82nd Airborne Division

I would like to talk about the policies and the conditions
of the people in our areas of operation. We had fire bases 20,
30 miles north of Saigon and we had one battalion on the
border. I was down there from January '69 to December '69.
This was about a year after the Tet Offensive and conditions
were quiet. There was some light contact, but the North Vietnamese, you know, could not stage anything right around this
area because it was too much. Peace prevailed around the
area and with relatively light security. We were getting work
done without harassment from the enemy.

We got to know some of the Vietnamese people as human
beings. We talked to them, with interpreters, and got to know
some of these old papa-sans—trash, as the Army says. I mean,
these people do have so much intelligence and wisdom that
it's just phenomenal. And you learn that they don't really
want much materially because they never had anything. All
they want is a chance for peace, to live off the land, raise
their children peacefully. In the past it's just been too much.

They never knew anything else besides this war. It's just tearing everything up. We cleared about 2000 acres north of Saigon, about 20 miles north, with many tunnels there, destroying the land.

Actually, atrocities were not too prevalent there because the Army felt it was close to a populated area and they didn't want any bad news. Just as the other man said, whenever the newsmen were around everything was nice. They went out of their way to keep calm. The Army didn't want any atrocities around this area. But we would go through one or two villages where they'd practice their explosives. Just walk into these huts and destroy one or two.

Sgt. John Beitzel, Americal Division

I'm 21. I was in Vietnam from January '69 to January '70. I served in the 11th Brigade, 4/21 Infantry. I served as a sergeant and as squad leader. Worked in Quang Ngai province. I worked around My Lai and Duc Pho.

I've witnessed the mutilation of bodies. This consisted of cutting off ears and plucking out teeth for souvenirs. I have pictures of this that I've showed to the press at other times. Don't have them with me today. I've witnessed electrical torture many times with not only VC suspects and prisoners, but also detainees. I've witnessed the relocation of villagers. One particular operation was a three day operation where we took all the villagers out of the village, put them in a barbed wire compound, interrogated them. Tortured some of them. Beat some of them. And then we had supplies brought in. Bangelore torpedoes, all types of explosives—to just level the ville and just get rid of anything; make it look like there was never a ville there. My CO once fired at a group of kids merely because they came up to our hill to collect C-rations. We were also ordered to fire gas grenades at them. There was a big pressure for body count. We had a very low body count in our company and we had a lot of pressure come down from the battalion commander to the company commander, down on to us. We were given new incentives to get a higher

83

body count such as a six-pack of beer or a case of soda. And sometimes, a three-day pass, you know, for the amount of body count we had.

Common things in my company were throwing grenades into civilian bunkers. We once threw a white phosphorous grenade. And a lot of times I never thought people were in these bunkers, but an old man came out when we threw this white phosphorous grenade in and he was all singed and burned. We—everywhere we went we would recon by fire if we felt . . . if we felt it necessary. We'd innumerable amount of free fire zones. We shot at anything on high ground. And in this particular area where I was at, the mountains and the high ground was very close to the beach. Was only a few miles between the beach and the high ground and there was a lot of hills, isolated hills, all over the place. We shot anything or anybody that went up on these hills. Because they were free fire zones.

Burning villages was very common. Villagers would leave and we suspected that they left because they were VC and they didn't want to be captured. So we would burn their ville. Whenever we received sniper fire we would return it, no matter where it came from. If it was a ville with people in it or not.

We were ordered to go out on a patrol—a regular patrol that we go on all the time—during a cease fire. We were very perturbed at this because we wanted to take the time off to write letters home. In one incident, we were working with another company and our battalion was nearby. Both companies were on the same radio frequency. Over the radio, the other company told us to pass on to our higher command that they had a body count of thirteen. So we passed it on up. (They were too far to have radio contact.) So we passed it on up. Then later, one of our platoons went into the village and they said we can confirm the body count of that company. They said, there's nine women, three children, and one baby.

As far as torturing the prisoners, this happened as . . . I've seen a major there during torturing of prisoners. We also had electrical field phones in our battalion base camp in the head-

quarters TOC room, that's what they call the headquarters.
There was torture going on in there so I'm as sure—I'm sure
everyone from battalion commander on down knew of it; so
I can presume from this, it was policy. These things I'm telling about—about burning the villages, free fire zones, reconning by fire—they were all common. They weren't isolated. We did them wherever we went.

Michael Kenny, 1st Marine Division

I joined the Marine Corps at the age of 17 in '68. Served
in Vietnam '69-'70, 2nd Battalion, 26th Marines. My testimony mainly concerns the maltreatment and murder of Vietnamese noncombatants and the general maltreatment of the
civilian population.

In many instances, particularly Operation Brave Armada,
which took place in Quang Ngai province in the summer of
'69, circumstances would come up where there would be a
patrol walking along, a single person or a small group of
persons would be sighted at a distance of anywhere from,
like, one to maybe five hundred meters. The standard procedure was to holler, "Dung Lai!" which is "Stop." A lot of
times the civilians or Vietnamese couldn't hear at that
distance and if they didn't respond immediately, the procedure was to have the squad or platoon open up on these
people. Upon approaching the bodies it was usually found
that these people had no weapons at all; that the only reason
they hadn't stopped was that they hadn't heard or were
frightened; and in order to explain these civilian bodies it was
standard procedure to carry several extra fragmentation
grenades in the field and these would be planted on the
bodies in order to make them a Viet Cong rather than a
civilian.

I understand from other people I have talked to that this
was fairly standard operating procedure. On several instances
the platoon commander, a lieutenant, actually ordered this to
be done. When a body was found, the general procedure was
that if the body didn't have a weapon it was a Viet Cong

85

suspect. If a weapon could be planted on it, it became a Viet
Cong, and if the body had any other equipment other than a
weapon, that is any piece of uniform or other equipment, it
became a North Vietnamese and this was the general criterion
that our battalion used to discriminate.

SP/4 William Rice, 9th Infantry Division

I'm from Vineland, New Jersey, I'm 21 years old. I was a
machine gunner for D Company, 3rd Battalion, 47th Infantry, and then when they were moved out I was transferred
to Headquarters, 3rd Brigade.

We had very little contact with prisoners, actually our
company never ran into too many of them. On occasions we
took detainees. Whether they were Viet Cong or not was not
determined at the time. Officers would take them and with
the Tiger Scout perform interrogations, field interrogations.
Sometimes including beatings. Other times the favorite
trick—especially in the Delta where you have a lot of water—
you just take him down to the water and dunk him a few
times until he starts talking. Just hold him down longer each
time, until he talks. That was the main way to get information from people. Now these were not confirmed VC. These
could have been civilians, because a lot of them were shipped
out on a helicopter later on, to detainee centers.

Our company was sweeping northeast of the city of Jon
Trong in Jon Trong district in Cam Hoa province, when we
came across this paddy. Our point element broke into this
paddy which was being worked by ten farmers. There were
old men and women with water buffalo and children working
in the field. They commenced to yelling "La De," which
means "Come here" in Vietnamese, and the people started
running when they saw the Americans. At this time someone
noticed a young man, of approximately military age, taking
off down a paddy dike. The point element opened up on him
and finally brought him down. He received a gunshot wound
in the head. The only thing he had was a transistor radio. We
come up to him and found the transistor. I do not know

whether he had an ID card or not. Our medic went up to him and started treating him. At this time we were ordered on up the road. I got about ten feet up the road and another member of my platoon said one of the sergeants had slit his throat.

We left the body laying on the dike, and went on. The transistor radio wound up in our hootch, where we used to listen to it.

SP/5 Michael Erard, 173rd Airborne Brigade

I served with the 3rd Battalion, 503rd Infantry and I had two jobs. I was in the field for about four months as a line doggie transferred into a battalion, and I served as the medic liaison with S-5. S-5 is what they call civil affairs to handle the PSY-OP operations, to handle the Chieu Hoi program for the battalion.

The Chieu Hoi program is designed to get NVA and VC defectors to come over to our side and the specific instructions given out on a battalion level were that these people were to be treated differently than POWs. If a man, after a contact or during a contact, would raise his hand and say Chieu Hoi, the Americans were supposed to give that man treatment. He was supposed to be set aside. He was supposed to be given receipts for his weapons. None of his personal belongings were to be touched. This was the battalion SOP, but it was never carried out on a company level. On my whole tour there our battalion never took a live Chieu Hoi. There were many leaflets dropped. We found Chieu Hoi passes on bodies of dead VC and dead NVA, but we never took a person in. The feeling among the grunts was that they didn't trust the Chieu Hoi.

I went down with an officer to Saigon, to the national Chieu Hoi center to recruit these former NVAs to serve as what we called Kit Carson Scouts. These scouts would serve in a line company. They would serve as the point men on the line companies. For the most part they were mistreated in the battalion. They were not given proper equipment. They were saying, well, a gook doesn't have to have this. A gook doesn't have to have that. He was supposed to have the exact complement that a U.S. soldier had in the field, but he never got it. The soldiers didn't want a Chieu Hoi, a Kit Carson, in their platoon. We had to force company commanders to take a Chieu Hoi into the company.

There were numerous accidents around our LZ, LZ Uplift, which is south of Bong Son, in Bin Dinh province. We had a friendly village to the south of us. There were two times when Americans fired from the perimeter into this village. Working in S-5 I would go out and be part of the investigating team in which the American government would investigate the accident. Then we would pay them what they called a "saladium payment." Now the saladium payment was a condolence type payment, like you might send flowers to someone's funeral. It in no way implied or implicated us as the perpetrators of this. So we would pay them a certain amount of money for people lost. In one incident there was a woman and five children killed and I think a sum of $500 was paid for this.

In another incident, right before I left, a young boy was out tending cattle. An M-79 was fired from the perimeter and he was seriously wounded. We could not take him to an American hospital. We spent about an hour just preparing him for surgery. He was not taken to an American hospital but to a Vietnamese hospital. This was battalion SOP, that you did not take wounded Vietnamese to American facilities. No payment was made and I went all the way to brigade on this. I tried to get payment for the family of this boy who died, but I was not able to follow it through. At the time I left, the S-5 officer there would not listen to me; the brigade S-5 would not listen to me.

The last thing that I want to relate was the last mission that I was involved in in Vietnam. Our battalion was in the An Lau Valley in Bin Dinh province, which is west of Bong Son. Our mission was to interdict NVA infiltration down the valley. I was the medic; I was the senior medic on Fire Base Abby. Along these valleys there were small garden plots and graves. In the garden plots were potatoes and small fruit-type gardens, or truck-type gardens. Intelligence said that the NVA were using these gardens as sources of food. In the period of six weeks that I was there, I know of ten civilians, ten unarmed civilians, who were killed tending these gardens. Again, I had access to the TOC and to all the briefings. The battalion CO was upset that there were no weapons found with these people. They were shot while they were working the field and there were no weapons found with the people. It was covered up on the battalion level and these people were reported as VC. In fact, they were old men who were killed working these plots.

Again, there were PSY-OP missions and Chieu Hoi passes were dropped in the area. But the fact was that these people were up there to visit graves. The graves were actually in the garden plots. I doubt very much if the people really understood that they weren't supposed to be in the area. The area was not a free fire zone. So prisoners were not taken.

In regard to medical treatment of wounded Vietnamese, and this involves not only captured prisoners, but also any Vietnamese, when we went out into the field we were issued a small bottle of serum albumin, about 500 cc's. Our platoon sergeant said, "This is worth $25. Never use it on a gook." There were many occasions where a wounded Vietnamese was sent back or dusted off with only a bandage to stop the bleeding when the man needed IV fluids to make it. He was not given that aid. We had to account for our bottles of serum albumin just as we had to account for our morphine. We were, we were not allowed to waste it on a Vietnamese.

SP/4 Gary Keyes, Americal Division

I was a Spec/4 when I was assigned to E troop, 1st Cav, Americal Division. I guess the worst thing I really saw over there was mistreatment of civilians. Now, most of this went on when we had convoys running from Duc Pho to Sai Wen. Such things as tear gassing villages, throwing spent 50-caliber rounds at civilians.

Sometimes, another instance, where children were with

89

split skulls from a thrown 50-caliber round. You can kill them just throwing them. Running down hootches. Doing things in rice paddies. Destroying their crops. The worst thing I ever really saw was when we're on a mission. We're taking some grunts out on a beachhead. And there were some fishermen out on the ocean and a couple of our sergeants thought it would be a good sport to use them as target practice. So they swung their 50-calibers around and they just shot the shit out of them, for no reason, I guess.

And, I'm no better. Lots of times on mine sweep, we'd pass a lake, also running from Duc Pho to Sai Wen, and there'd be fishermen in this lake and since we had nothing better to do, we'd fire M-79 rounds at them, M-16 rounds. Sometimes M-60s. We'd call for a test fire. And . . . sort of aim their way, hoping we'd hit somebody. I can't really say why we did it. Maybe it was because we were taught to hate them. I know this is all I heard when I was over there. I was told by my own lieutenant, my XO [Executive Officer], well, he saw me wearing one of these bracelets—you've probably seen them before. Well, a Vietnamese boy gave it to me and we were pretty uptight, you know. I thought he was a pretty neat little kid. And first thing he did was, he told me, he asked asked me why I was wearing it. I told him, I said, "Well, a Vietnamese boy gave it to me." I said it was a token of his friendship, really. He liked me and I liked him. We gave each other gifts, I suppose. And, he told me to take it off. And, of course, I didn't agree. I didn't want to take it off. I didn't feel I should. But, he told me these are the same people—he says, "Why do you accept gifts from the same people that go out and put mines in the roads and blow up your buddies?" And he told me that if I didn't take it off, he'd go to more maybe drastic measures, I don't know. And he just dismissed me. But, I don't know. I don't want to give any blood stories or nothing. I just can't do it. I just want you to know that the people over there aren't really being treated as human beings. They're being treated as slaves, let's say. Maybe not even slaves. I don't know. I don't know. I just don't know what to say. I just wanted you to know about it.

L/Cpl. Robert Clark, 3rd Marine Division

I'm 22 years old. Right after high school I entered the Marine Corps. I served as a Battalion Radio Operator and interpreter with Golf Company 2/9 from May to August 1969. From December 1969 to late February '70 I served as One Four Chief calling in air strikes in Vietnam. I'm currently unemployed and a resident of Philadelphia. My testimony will concern killing of wounded prisoners, prisoner refused medical attention and as a result died with about 30 Marines watching him including a colonel, brutalities toward Vietnamese children and women.

I served with Golf Company, 2/9, and due to my popularity and quick mouth in the company, I made frequent garbage runs. We were instructed that when we got down there that if anybody was going through the garbage, chase them away; we could do what we wanted to do and if anybody jumped on the truck they were fair game for anything. Now what they did, they put about ten grunts on the truck and they just laid down in the garbage and we'd have two standing on the back of the truck. Now when about 30 people would jump on the truck, then the ten grunts would jump off and they'd just beat 'em with their rifle clubs until they were either knocked senseless and then they'd knock 'em on the ground and just kick their ass all the way across the garbage dump, which was over a hundred yards long. At the time I was there, nobody ever got hurt in the garbage dump as far as Americans. But a lot of Vietnamese women and children were hurt.

And it was fair game between Con Thien and going through the city of Cam Lo, on the outskirts of Quang Tri going into Stud, that American troops would stock up on their heavies (their spaghetti and meatballs, and ham and lima beans) and any little children who were begging along the side of the road, which never numbered less than 50 or 60, were fair game for these full cans of food. They wouldn't throw them to the kids, they would just bounce them off their heads or try and knock them off their bicycles. If they

91

ran out of food, they would just light up heat tabs and wait until a kid got really close to the truck and then they would just easily drop it into his hands.

And particularly this Bru village they relocated them right on Route 9 right close to the Rockpile. And there was a little kid with crutches out there—he was missing one leg—he was about five years old and he was about the most popular target because every time we came by he ran out and the people wanted to see if they could knock his crutch or hit his old man in his woods, because if the kid ever did get any candy, he brought it to his old man and these two people were the most popular targets.

Moderator: You mentioned the killing of wounded prisoners. Would you talk about that also?

Clark: Right on. On June 13th, on Operation Cannon Falls, we were on Fire Support Base Wisemans, Golf Company and H and S Company. Now at 2:30 in the morning I was used as a line filler because one of our listening posts was wiped out and they had to send a platoon of grunts out there to see who was alive and who was dead. At three o'clock, we were hit by exactly a company and a half and the contact lasted until five-thirty. We were hit with RPGs and small rifle fire plus they threw some Chicoms, but everybody forgot to pull the pins so none of them went off. Now twice during the night we were overrun on our lower LP. The whole night we only sustained three dead people and ten wounded. Now in the morning when the mist cleared, about five-thirty, everybody just got out of their holes and we started to sweep down towards the bottom of the hill to count our body count and see how brave we were. There was one NVA soldier who was caught on the wire. He had a bullet wound through the neck and numerous shrapnel wounds all through his body from fragmentation grenades. Now this big bad-assed corporal took out his knife and stuck it in his neck and just jiggled it until the man bled to death because he didn't want to carry him to the top of the hill. Another man was laying at the bottom of the hill on his stomach. He was in pretty bad shape but I think he would have made it and three grunts emptied full magazines of M-16 fire in his back.

92

Another man who was shot at the top of the hill and had a bullet wound in his thigh, two in his back, and his elbow was hanging off by a thread, plus he had numerous shrapnel wounds from fragmentation grenades. He was laying on his back at the top of the hill and what was left of second platoon and first platoon gathered around him including a lieutenant colonel, a major, a captain, and at least one 2nd lieutenant. He was made the object of a little game for about a half hour. He was screaming for water and they just poured it on the ground. They laughed at him; they kicked him in the ribs. One time he just jumped up spastically and he sat up on his waist and his arms started to dangle. A grunt kicked him in the chest and he died. While all this was going on, they were suggesting what they should do with him. There were three senior squids there—that's doctors—all three of them were E-6s, none of them would help him. They said, "He's not worth it." Somebody suggested we tie him up because he might be dangerous. It was suggested he might be tied up with barbed wire.

Now after all this happened, they chased what was left of the NVA company out through the woods and an NVA lieutenant surrendered. He ran to the bottom of the hill and he walked up with a Chieu Hoi leaflet to the gunnery sergeant. He was unarmed; he didn't have anything on him; he grabbed the gunnery sergeant's hand and kissed it and he seemed pretty happy. Well, he got punched out. They brought him up to the top of the hill and he wasn't physically abused because he told everything he knew, plus he got on a loud speaker, and he talked through a helicopter that was circling the area telling his comrades to surrender. Well, that night he said that we were going to be hit with 60 mortar fire and it was going to march from the east side of the hill to the west side. They decided to keep him there overnight so they took off all his clothes and they dug him a little hole, three feet by four feet. They just put him in there and put a board on top and had the Kit Carson sleep on top, just in case we didn't get hit by the mortar fire then they would take care of him. Well, we did get hit by the mortar fire and we took care of him anyhow.

Capt. John Mallory, 1st Air Cavalry Division

I served as a captain with the 11th Armored Cavalry Regiment, which during most of my time in Vietnam from May 1969 to May 1970, was under the operational control of the 1st Air Cavalry Division. I served as Regimental Assistant Civic Action Officer and Civic Action Officer for the 1st Squadron, 11th Armored Cav.

I'd like to say a few words about treatment of Vietnamese civilians by members of the 11th Armored Cavalry Regiment. The destruction of crops and killing of domestic animals was common whenever the 11th Armored Cavalry Regiment operated in populated areas. Crops were destroyed in the building of defensive positions and animals were run over when the tracks—armored cars, tanks—ran through the villages. Civilian deaths were quite frequent, Vietnamese civilians were killed accidentally when tracks and tanks running through their villages, often at excessive speeds, struck them, ran off the road, ran into their houses, hit their bicycles, etc. On at least one occasion, the village of An Phu in Binh Long province was struck by artillery fired from Quan Loi base camp causing several casualties. A civilian riding on an ox cart, just south of Quan Loi base camp, was intentionally struck by an American aircraft which came in out of the sky, hit him in the head, and traveled on. The man was killed; the aircraft was never identified. A helicopter, also never identified, dropped two white phosphorous grenades (they're incendiary grenades) into the village of Sa Troc, also in Binh Long province, burning down several buildings and two small Montagnard children. In Loc Ninh, a young boy about 12 years old was attacked by two American soldiers, severely beaten, resulting in a broken arm. There is no reason known for this attack.

On one occasion, a North Vietnamese Army nurse was killed by 11th Armored Cavalry troops; subsequently a grease gun of the type used in automotive work was placed in her vagina and she was packed full of grease. On several occasions, enemy graves were violated, their skulls taken out of the graves and used as candle holders and conversation pieces.

94

CS gas, better known as tear gas, was often used on civilians to chase them away from our positions where they came to sell, or to look for valuable American trash in our trash dumps. On one occasion, this gassing of Vietnamese civilians was done by an American Army major. On another occasion, Vietnamese selling their wares in the area had their wares taken and destroyed by American troops led by two captains. One of them was myself. In August, in Binh Long province, north of An Loc, six Vietnamese (friendly Vietnamese soldiers or civilians or regular Defense Group soldiers) were killed by helicopter gun ships from the 11th Armored Cavalry Regiment. Although the CIDG area of operations was clearly marked on our tactical map in our tactical operations center, sheer carelessness of the duty officer from the 11th Armored Cav led him to give our gun ships permission to fire at armed Vietnamese in the area, although it was quite well known that there were friendly armed Vietnamese in that immediate vicinity.

In general, U.S. attitudes towards Vietnamese civilians were not inhumane per se, but they were certainly not human. The Vietnamese civilians were regarded much as America regards her own minorities—a pat on the head for a trick, a kick in the ass for an imagined fault, and invisible the rest of the time.

HM3 Jeff Dubrow, 1st Medical Battalion

I was a Hospital Corpsman on the USS Sanctuary in Da Nang. I worked in the surgical unit on board the Sanctuary. And most of the minor surgical procedures that were done on the Sanctuary were done in the recovery room. Such as debridement of wounds around minor suturing cases, things like that.

An ARVN soldier came in one day. I set him up for his procedure. It was a debridement of a wound and it's done under a local anesthesia, like xylocaine or novocaine. I set the tray out and I drew up 10 cc's of xylocaine. The ARVN was pretty apprehensive about what was going to be happening to him. So we had the interpreter tell him what was going on and he calmed down. About five, ten minutes later he was screaming like crazy, you know. I ran over to see what was the matter and I noticed that the syringe hadn't been touched, and the doctor was performing this procedure without anesthesia. He had done this about ten times. I've seen him do it. And he was a lieutenant commander, by the way, which is like a major, so he knew better. Also the same doctor claimed in some cases he was rushed, like from one case to another. Like in suturing cases, I've seen him perform suturing cases without the use of sterile technique. In other words, no gloves. And it only takes 15 seconds to put a glove on, you know. So there was no excuse for that. This is, like I said, done only on ARVN soldiers, not American soldiers.

Another doctor, who was a lieutenant commander also, performed 27 out of 30 negative laparotomy cases. A laparotomy is cutting into the abdomen and exposing the intestines and repairing any tear or wound that would be in the intestines. The x-rays would come in with the patient from triage, or from x-ray, or wherever, and I put the x-rays up on the screen. So I saw every x-ray that came in on these patients. And you could see a metal fragment in the intestines. It stands out like a sore thumb. It's just like a big, you know, lump in the middle of nothing. You can really see it.

If, let's say, an ARVN or Vietnamese civilian would come in with a fragment wound of the arm or leg, or something like that, he would automatically order a laparotomy to be set up on him. We can't question him because I'm only an E-4 and he was a lieutenant commander. So I had to do what I was told. So, he would do these cases that didn't have to be done and a laparotomy can be an easy case. If there's a frag there, he could take the frag out, repair the wound and that's it. Sometimes it can be a very bad case. There would be a lot of bleeding done. I've seen fellows from a simple fragment of the stomach, die in surgery. And he would do these cases and they wouldn't have to be done. And like I say, there was 27 out of 30 negative cases. That's about all I have to say.

Sgt. Gary Steiger, 366th Air Force Dispensary

I served as a Medic in the 366th USAF Dispensary at Da
Nang. We worked six days a week in Vietnam in our dispensary. And you can get pretty bored on your days off because
there really wasn't a heck of a lot to do. And there were, I
think, six hospitals in the area including the ship that Jeff
was on. Oftentimes the Air Force's medics would go to the
navy or marine hospital. I worked quite a bit in those places,
and triage is a system whereby the patients are divided into
three main categories for treatment. If you have a person
coming in who is really badly wounded—he may have a limb
or two missing, or multiple shrapnel wounds or whatever, and
they expect him to die—he's placed in a category "expectant." Right after those people come the guys that if they
weren't treated immediately would possibly die. In the "expectant" category, the chances are they wouldn't make it
even with surgery. And the third category is a delay, in which
the guys come in, maybe have minor wounds, or things like
this.

When patients came in, not only to the navy hospitals
and others, but when they came in to our casualty staging
flight where I worked, these patients would usually be the
ones that were treated last. You could have an American
come in in an expectant category and there was no way that
he was going to make it. And the doctors would oftentimes
treat him before they would treat an ARVN soldier or NLF
soldier, or whatever, in a lower category who had a really
good chance of making it if he was taken care of. Most of the
time the corpsmen would give him basic first aid and that was
it. You weren't supposed to use any more of your supplies on
them than was absolutely necessary to get them out of your
facility and into a Vietnamese hospital.

Now the prisoners that I saw that we handled were taken
into our hospitals where they didn't receive treatment. I
mean, it's, it's no way to . . . I, I lose the words. I mean they
were lower than worms as far as these people were concerned. I mean you don't treat worms and you don't treat
ARVN. It was about the same thing. We'd bring them in on a

97

Medivac. The Air Force flies cargo planes. They're hooked up for carrying litters and they carry wounded personnel and so forth on them. A C-130 would come in which could maybe carry 60 American wounded, and it would have over 100 Vietnamese on it. *Well* over 100. Stacked on top of each other and everything else. These people'd get off. They'd be taken off the plane. You'd have a man who's say in a body cast—you know, cast from his neck to his knees—and he'd be walking down the ramp and somebody would trip. This guy would fall three feet. He'd maybe had half the bones in his body broken and the doctor'd spent hours in OR working on him, and they'd drop him from three feet. They'd put them into buses, and they were tossed into the buses more than put. They would take them down to the ARVN hospitals instead of taking them to a place where they could be treated. They'd be taken there and even if the ARVN didn't have the facilities—which they don't have—to treat these patients, we'd leave them anyway.

The prisoners were transferred. There's several hospitals where they take care of these. And it was common knowledge amongst the people that were working on the flight line transferring these prisoners that they were turned over to the Koreans. It was a standing joke that in the Korean hospital if you had a patient who was really bad off, and you were sending someone down there who wasn't quite so bad off, and they didn't have the beds, the one in the bed that was going to die anyway would either be shot or something else done to them, so they'd have room. And this happened all the time.

The patients that we got in our casualty staging flight would set up in the end of the ward; if you were lucky, you could give them some water. It wasn't worth your time to treat them. That's the way I saw it. Unless we can realize that those people are human beings, that we're killing human beings over there, that they are the same flesh and blood of which we are . . . I don't know. We're just not human beings ourselves.

Sgt. Ted Eckert, 1st Marine Division

I'm 21 years old and I'm a resident of Las Vegas, Nevada. I entered the Marine Corps in March 1968 and was sent to Nam July of the following year. I was attached to Marine Wing Support Group 17, 1st Marine Air Wing. My testimony deals with harassment fire from the air, burning of villages from the air, and black marketeering in Da Nang itself.

I was up in Quang Tri visiting a friend of mine who was on security, which is like a rat patrol. They go out in these little jeeps and patrol the perimeter. We were out about five o'clock in the morning just about coming in, when they spotted this old woman about—she looked about fifty but she was probably about twenty-five—and she was running across some trees and everyone in the jeep—no one was supposed to be out there, of course—it was not a free fire zone, but from the hours from dusk to dawn there's not supposed to be anybody out there, and if there is, you're supposed to stop them, check them out, and eliminate them if you have to. So these guys decided that they would kind of play a little game and they let her run about fifty yards and they'd fire in front of her so she'd have to turn around, and then they'd let her run another direction and then they'd cut her off. This went on about a half hour until the time the sun started to come up. So then they decided it best to eliminate her as soon as possible, so they just ripped her off right there and then the guy, the corporal that was in charge, he decided that they'd better check her out for an ID card just to be safe about it and they went over and, of course, she didn't have an ID card; she didn't have anything. Her only crime was being out probably tending to her buffalo before the time she should have been. These guys just took it upon themselves to waste her.

I think the feeling was pretty widespread that these people were inferior to us, and based on the training we received these people were not looked upon as even humans. If they had slanted eyes they were the enemy and the only good one was a dead one. And that was for the majority of the people in my unit, that was the only way they looked at it.

99

Major David Galicia, 3rd Field Hospital

The last thing I think I'd like to add to this is to tell you an experience that I had. I can't document this because I don't know the dates. I know the places, but I don't know the dates and I don't know the names. But because of my traveling and because of my rank (I was a major at that time) and maybe perhaps because of my personality, I got into multiple places where now, when I think about it, I had no business being. But I got invitations to just about every place. And one night I was down with the last element of the 9th Infantry Division that was left in country at that time, the 3rd Brigade, who had four battalions left. They each had their base camp areas. The brigade headquarters was located at Tan An, which was about 40 miles south of Saigon. I was asked if I would like to take a tour of the tactical operations center, or the TOC. I said I thought that would be a real good idea. I tried to figure in my mind what I thought it would be like in there and I thought there's probably a bunch of relief maps, situational maps, banks of radios, telephones, and a lot of people. When I got in there, I found that my assessment was pretty good; that's about what it was. Except for the fact that when I started looking around, I noticed that there were four charts on this wall, on opposite walls, and each one of these charts had recorded on it for an entire year the monthly kill, one battalion against another, like it was a game. It is off these kind of things, I'm certain, that rank is made. The most upsetting thing was the way it was condoned. While I was there, they were in contact out in the field with someone, and apparently pretty good contact. In the presence of this major, who was running it, a bell rang three times. I asked him what that was all about and he said, "We just killed three of theirs." I looked at the man, turned around, and said, "Man, what the hell do you do when they kill one of ours?" He had no answer for me and this was the end of our conversation.

IV. "TORTURING IS JUST ANOTHER WAY . . ."

SP/4 Steve Noetzel, 5th Special Forces Group Augmentation

I'm from Floral Park, Long Island, New York. I was drafted in 1962, in July. I went to Vietnam June of 1963 and stayed until May of 1964. While in Vietnam, I was attached to the 5th Special Forces Group. I was a member of a psychological warfare civic action team. While in Vietnam I traveled extensively through the Mekong Delta with our psy war efforts, and during this time I witnessed several incidents of mistreatment, maltreatment, of prisoners and that's what I'm here to testify about today. I now work for the Bell System. I'm in management at their headquarters in New York.

The first incident that I will speak about happened in November or December of 1963. I was stationed in Can Tho in the Mekong Delta and was trying to hitchhike a chopper ride to Saigon. The only flight going to Saigon on that particular day was a five-chopper flight. They were transporting some 16 prisoners, South Vietnamese prisoners, who had been interrogated at several levels before being sent to Saigon. They were transporting these prisoners in two helicopters, double-rotor helicopters, H-121. There were eight prisoners brought onto each helicopter. They were tied, their hands were tied behind their backs, and they were tethered together with rope around their necks, and about a six-foot length of rope to the next prisoner. A string of eight of them like that were put on each helicopter. With them were about an equal number of South Vietnamese or ARVN troops as guards. Also on that flight of five helicopters were three gun ships, HUIB single-rotor helicopters. I flew in the first of these helicopters. The point helicopter. We were to fly support for this mission to bring these prisoners to Saigon. Incidentally, during those days, prisoners were brought to Saigon for a six-month rehabilitation program and then they were released after the six months to go back to wherever

101

they wanted to go—that is, South Vietnamese or NLF prisoners.

We took off from Can Tho. We heard—or I heard (I had a headset on)—the radio message to Saigon. We got in contact with MACV headquarters in Saigon, told them we were coming with 16 prisoners, and they said they would have a greeting party for us at Tan Son Nhut Airport. We flew in one direct, nonstop flight. All the ships stayed together the entire flight, about an hour and ten minutes or so. No helicopter left the group at any time. It could never have caught up with us if it did leave and land anywhere. We landed in Saigon. I got out of the helicopter, and there was a greeting party there to meet us, a colonel from MACV and some other field grade officers. They had a paddy wagon to transport prisoners and so on. When we got off the helicopter, there were exactly three prisoners left on one helicopter, and one prisoner left on the other helicopter. These prisoners were now bound with their hands behind their backs. They were blindfolded, and of course no tether or no rope around their necks attaching to any other prisoners. I instantly realized what had happened and couldn't believe it, although I knew, rationally, what *had* to have happened.

I went over to the American door gunner of one of the transport ships, and I asked him what the hell happened, and he told me that they had pushed them out over the Mekong Delta. And I said, "Who?" and he said, "The ARVN guards did." And I just shook my head and said, "I can't believe it," and he said, "Go over there and look at the doorway." There are open doorways on these helicopters; they have no closable door, there's just a door frame. And I went over to the doorway and stopped when I got about five feet away and didn't want to go any closer because there was flesh from the hands of the prisoners when they were pushed out on the door jambs and on the door frames. And there was blood on the floor where they had been beaten and pushed out of the helicopters.

I went back to my own helicopter that I had just gotten out of and there I overheard the conversation between the American pilots and the MACV colonel who had come to meet the prisoners, and he asked them what the hell happened to the other prisoners and one of the American pilots simply said to him, "They tried to escape over the Mekong Delta." That was the first, or only, incident of helicopter murder that I had seen in Vietnam.

Moderator: Steve, could you now relate to treatment of prisoners at a specific A Team camp or in the Delta?

Noetzel: Right. This occurred at one particular camp, this was an A Team at a place called Tan Phu which is in the Caman Peninsula, deep in the Mekong Delta, the southernmost A Team. It was in a completely isolated area. It was completely VC controlled (around the A Team camp). In January or February of 1964, I'm not sure exactly which month, I witnessed an almost public, or not almost, a public display of electrical torture of Vietnamese prisoners.

The way the camp was situated, it had about four- or five-foot walls around the compound, maybe even a little higher than that. There were at least 100 or 150 ARVN strike forces watching from inside the compound, all of the American A Team that was there was watching, and also there was a little bridge at a canal right next to the camp, a little camelback bridge, and if you stood at the middle of the bridge, on the highest part of it, you could see down into the camp. And the torture was done outside at a place in the camp where anyone standing on the bridge could watch it. It was done for psychological effect, I suppose, to show off a new invention, or a new kind of lie detector that they had conjured up.

A captain there, the commander of the A Team, had conjured up a system of electrical torture whereby they took a Sony tape recorder, a plain tape recorder with the U-meters on it, and hooked that up with some field telephone batteries (hooked up in series) and a toggle switch, that was held under the table by a Special Forces sergeant. Then the captain asked questions of a prisoner, who was stripped naked, and electrodes from these field telephones were attached to the back of his neck, to his armpits, to his genitals, and his feet. He was told that this apparatus was a lie detector, that he would be interrogated, and that every time he didn't tell the truth, the machine would give him a shock. He didn't know the difference between a lie detector, or had never seen a tape recorder, I guess. In truth, the captain simply asked questions and the interpreter asked them in Vietnamese. When the captain didn't like the answer, he gave some kind of signal to the sergeant, who gave him an electrical charge and the fellow would jump and scream.

Everyone was very impressed with this new lie detector, except, I guess, the fellow who was being questioned and couldn't understand why the lie detector was working so badly. He may or may not have been telling the truth. At any rate, they got information. Whether it was valid or not, I don't know.

At the B Team in Can Tho, this was the headquarters for the Four Corps, they had an eight-foot python snake which was kept at the camp in a cage, supposedly for rat control. When we had prisoners or detainees who were brought to the B Team, they were immediately questioned, and if they balked at all or sounded like they weren't going to be co-operative, they were simply placed in a room overnight. This was like a detention room; the door was locked, and this snake was thrown in there with them. Now the python is a constrictor, similar to a boa. It's not poisonous. It will snap at you, but it's not poisonous, and it probably can't kill a full-grown American or a large male, but it sure terrified the Vietnamese. Two of them usually in a room overnight with the python snake, struggling with it most the night, I guess, and we could hear them screaming. In fact, on one instance, they had to go in there and gag the prisoners, so they wouldn't keep everyone awake all night. In the morning they were usually more cooperative.

I didn't see any humane treatment of prisoners, but I didn't see that many prisoners. However, every time I did see them, they were being mistreated in one way or another. If it wasn't electrical torture, it was the snake torture. If it wasn't the snake torture, it was barbed wire cages, which are also used in Tan Phu. This was a coffin-like cage made of barbed wire, about the shape of a coffin—barbed wire strung around stakes. A prisoner was stripped naked and put into this cage for about a 24-hour period. In the daytime he would bake in the sun, and in the night the mosquitoes would eat him all night, I guess. If the mosquitoes weren't particularly attracted to the Orientals, which they're not, they were sprayed with some kind of a mosquito-attracting liquid, and they'd be full of bites in the morning.

Finally, if it wasn't that, at the B Team at Can Tho, there was another form of torture, a water torture. Prisoners were taken, usually two in a small canoe, out behind the compound in a small rice paddy. They were bound, their hands behind their back. They were blindfolded and were put on this little canoe. An American Special Forces sergeant was there, another Vietnamese soldier was there, and they poled the boat around in circles in this rice paddy. Except that it wasn't a rice paddy any more, it had been a rice paddy. Now it was used as a latrine, really. There's where the drainage from the B Team latrines went, into this rice paddy. It was filled with urine and feces, and it stank to high heaven. The prisoners were rowed around in that water and were asked questions. And when they balked, the fellow who was poling the boat simply took the pole and knocked them out of the boat into this water where they sputtered around for a few minutes. It was about four feet deep or so. They were blindfolded with hands tied behind their back. Finally they surfaced somehow, after drinking half of it, I guess, and were dragged back into the canoe. That was about the only kind of treatment of prisoners I saw.

Sgt. Fred Nienke, 1st Marine Division

We took a lot of prisoners. Some of them were suspected VC, NVA, and they were usually brought to the compound, when we took prisoners, and turned over to an interpreter, usually a South Vietnamese or Korean interpreter, and if the information couldn't be extracted from them they were tortured and sent back to the CP, the Command Post.

Moderator: What type of torture was used? Would you know?

Nienke: Well, we were basically on the lines and we could hear screaming. I didn't see any torture, but we could hear screaming and somebody was being beaten. I ran into some prisoners that tried to surrender but we were a roving battalion in Vietnam and we went to a lot of different places, mostly way out in the bush, up in the mountains, not close to any major Army or Marine bases such as this, and we didn't believe in Chieu Hois. We didn't take prisoners. When we did take prisoners, like, we'd come into a village and there might have been somebody that we thought could have possibly been a prisoner or a POW or a VC, whether it might be an old lady or a young kid or something like this, they were always brought back to our local platoon or CO position where we set up that night and interrogated.

Moderator: Did you ever witness any of this interrogation?

Nienke: Like I said before, we were mostly on the lines and I walked back—I'm not sure what province this was in—I walked back to talk to the captain because I was going on a listening post that night and I saw a young man and he was being beaten by an ARVN interpreter that came along with us. He was being beaten and I was told to leave the area.

Capt. Ernie Sachs, 1st Marine Division

This was one of the big games. Whenever any prisoners were taken, the crewmen in the helicopters who were in charge also of loading in addition to maintenance on the aircraft would blindfold the prisoners, holding the blindfold on with heavy wire, safety wire. They'd bind their hands, bind their feet, and maybe bind them into a fetal position and upon landing rather than releasing them so they could walk off the aircraft, they'd throw them out—get the grunts to mark how far they could throw them and have little contests. This was done with officers observing, at least all company grade officers. There may have been a major present too. The general attitude of the officers was (I was a lieutenant at the time) "Well, there's somebody senior to me here and I guess if this wasn't SOP he'd be doing something to stop it and since nobody senior ever did anything to stop it, the policy was promulgated and everybody assumed that this was what was right. We'd never had any instructions in the Geneva Conventions. When we were given our Geneva Convention cards the lecture consisted of "If you're taken prisoner, all you gotta do is give 'em your name, rank, serial number, and date of birth. Here's your Geneva Convention cards. Go get 'em, Marines." We were never told anything about the way to treat prisoners if we were the capturers rather than the captee and this was very standard.

It was an official policy that after every mission you fly, you have to fill out an after-mission report to show them all the good stuff you did during the day. Like, how many pounds of rice you carried, and how many Americans and how many gooks you carried. Well, we were given very specific oral orders from the colonel on down: When you are carrying VCs—Viet Cong suspects—you don't count them when you get in the airplane, you count them when they get out of the airplane because the numbers don't always jibe. And if one of them happens to get scared of heights and decides to get out, or something like that, or if he looks like maybe he's going to try and raise some shit in the belly of the aircraft and the crewman has to kick him out, that's none of your business; it didn't really happen because you counted the men when they got off.

Sgt. Murphy Lloyd, 173rd Airborne Brigade

Well, first of all we would ask them. If we didn't get the information, or if they said they didn't know any and we figured they were lying, we'd go to torture. The first time I ever saw it used was on Operation Junction City. We were over by the Cambodian border in War Zone C. We had just walked into an ambush, and out of this ambush we had approximately fifteen casualties. Five were killed out of those fifteen. We picked up five or six prisoners, and were flying them back toward our fire support base.

We had a lieutenant that had been in country about five days. He said that he was going to conduct the interrogation.

107

We were explaining to him that we had qualified people in the rear to do this, but he told us to shut up, he was a lieutenant. So boom, that ended that. So he asked two or three questions, and all of them kept saying "No bic" or "Mu la" or something—Either "I'm not going to tell you" or "I don't know." I believe it's "I don't know." So what he did, we were in a Chinook. A Chinook is bigger than a Huey. It has a door that opens in the rear and that's how we went in. Also it has a middle door used to take up cargo. Then he ordered the door opened, the middle door, and without another word, he just pushed one out. And then he said, "Are you going to tell me now?" and he started to put his gun on them. So all this time we're looking at him. We're kind of mad too because we had been out there and some of our friends had been killed or wounded. At the time it really didn't mean anything to us. He pushed out another one. Now the third one he came to, he started to say something in Vietnamese and pointed to one of them on the end. As we found out after searching this fellow, he was a lieutenant in the North Vietnamese Army. On the way in after this, he said if anything was said about this he would make it harder on us. Okay, so he wrote himself up for a medal by detaining and getting information from prisoners and saving us from walking into another ambush, evidently. But he received a Bronze Star with a V device in it for valor. The V stood for valor.

And again, we were in the northern part. We were up by Dak To. This was in May of 1967. A Company of the 2nd Battalion was annihilated, all but about four or five people. During the time that they were being annihilated up there, we were sitting down ready. Our battalion commander kept asking for word to go up. And the battalion commander of A Company, 2nd Battalion, kept saying they could hold their own, they could hold their own. So about four or five hours later they told us to saddle up and we had to go. They took us in on another side of the hill which was hot.

By the time we worked our way to where A Company [was] the airstrip was overrun by NVAs. They came through the old An Khe village side. The only ones left back there to defend it was the finance personnel, the clerks, and the cooks, more or less administrative people. So they took all the infantry people that were going home, issued us weapons right quick. They ran us on out to the airstrip. During this time we had worked our way across the airstrip, and after we got everything organized and we finally took back the airstrip, we started going on little search and destroy missions in old An Khe. We ran into a few NVA that came to us Chieu Hoi and right on the spot where we're taking them prisoner a lieutenant came up. He said, "There's a three-day pass for any body. If you can prove that you've killed an NVA you have a three-day pass to Vuc To"—that's the in-country R & R center. And right there at that point I actually with my own eyes saw a first sergeant and a lieutenant fight over who (the prisoners were killed; they were taken and killed right there on the spot), over who killed them. They just started to fight right there. And there's been quite a few incidents like that that I could recall.

I have helped in torturing prisoners. One time the village chief came and said that he wanted to take the bodies and put them on display in Sin City, where most of the soldiers went for entertainment. So that the rest of the people in the village, Viet Cong, NVA, would see 'em and leave. But he couldn't do this due to the fact that the majority of the bodies that were there that day either had their pinky finger joint cut off or their ears cut off. And at one time (we thought it was showing courage and bravery, or whatever you want to call it) we wore ears. We'd take them and catch them while they were alive. Take an ear. The Vietnamese people believe if they die without all of their bodies they won't go to heaven and we would do this to two or three of them to get information from the rest of them.

L/Cpl. David Bishop, 1st Marine Division

I was attached to Hotel Company 2/5. Before I went into the Marine Corps I was a lab technician. I'm still a lab technician.

This would have been on operation in Quang Nam

109

province between August and September of '69. We had just gone on a search and destroy mission in the mountains and we made no contact. We were on our way back and we knew of enemy in the area. There was a lot of rock formations where we were and we were checking out the bunkers and the holes and everything in the rocks and we came across a wounded prisoner who was a wounded Vietnamese. He appeared to be VC or NVA. He didn't have a weapon. There were a few grenades and rounds laying around him. He seemed to have been in this hole for quite a few days. One of his legs was broken in half and the maggots had already gotten into one of his legs and they were living inside his leg while he was still alive.

Well, we dragged him out and we had quite a distance to go down the mountain to get back to the base camp and the squad that found him had to report him to the skipper. The skipper came down to where they had found the prisoner, had asked the people around him to get going and that he would tend to the prisoner. I was machine gunner at the time and I had to set up some security around him and I came up over a rock to watch what he was doing and he took out his 45 and he blew his head off.

This, like, wasn't really the first time this ever happened. This happened quite a few times during this operation because we were working in the mountains and any POWs that we had it was really hard to get them back down the mountains and it was the general consensus of everyone that there would be no POWs. That any people that we did find would be KIAs and they were reported as such. They weren't reported as POWs. I hardly saw any Medivacs at all taking out wounded Vietnamese civilians or Vietnamese prisoners. Usually we didn't have any prisoners. The prisoners were exterminated.

Barry Hopkins, 9th Infantry Division

I'm 22 years old, from Greensberg, Kansas. I enlisted for the draft in '68 and went to Vietnam in January 1969 to

110

January '70. I was with the 3rd/39th, 9th Division. I was a point man for five months.

I think it was in April. I don't remember the province. It was pretty close to our fire base—Fire Base Moore. They reported that they had seen six VC. They eagle-flighted us in there and we started coming in on these hootches. It was wide open and there were a lot of hootches. We started going to each one and there were about five or six VC in each one. They were all real young, like about 18, 19 years old. We got 32 prisoners. They reported that there were that many and just a few more that were killed by the helicopters and our own men. I think they divided them up so we could have those evenly. There was more VC there than what they thought. The major came in and he and I witnessed one of my friends chasing one of these kids. He stabbed him and the kid just didn't want to die. So he took him in the moat and drowned him, and it took a long time to drown him. He just didn't want to die.

I couldn't dig going out, walking all that ways, and bringing in all these prisoners like these other guys. I just stuck around where the major was and was helping tag all the prisoners that they brought up. We used wire and string, wrote a number on it, and tied it around their necks to tag them. We had six women that we brought in. Some of my friends were really messing around with these women. There was a lot of mistreatment. We stood there and watched these leeches on these peoples' backs. They would suck out enough blood (they would be about five inches long) and these young guys would just fall over and nothing was done, and the major was standing right there. He observed us tying these tags around their necks and lot of the mishandling of the women and the young men.

Cpl. David Fortin, 3rd Marine Division

I served as the driver for the 3rd Medical Battalion, 3rd Marine Division in Quang Tri.

A prisoner would be brought into triage, which is where

111

they get their basic medical treatment before they go on to their specific needs like operations, which had to be performed directly by a doctor. Well, in triage, a prisoner would be interrogated. They'd come down with ITT, which is Intelligence Translations people, and they'd try to get information from the prisoners. If the prisoner wouldn't give information out to the questions they asked, they'd use various ways of torture. They'd poke at his wounds. I've seen them stand a prisoner up who had a stomach wound; his shoulder was torn up.

They generally harassed the prisoner until they could get information out of him. I don't even think he could speak. He was in pretty bad shape. They took him to an operating room and in the operating room he wasn't treated by a doctor, such as Americans were. I know sterile conditions were less than normal in this case. Rather than having a doctor who would work on an American, they'd have corpsmen who were practicing or getting experience from working on the prisoners, treat them. He was in pretty bad shape. They had very little regard, whatsoever, for the concern of him once they got him out of the operating room. Their attitude was like, okay, we got to do it so we're going to do it, you know. But, like, who cares whether he lives or dies. It's just something that has to be done. There was one doctor present. Other than that, the corpsmen did all the major work. They set bones, very sloppily. If you set a bone sloppily, it's going to come out crooked. They don't care.

You've heard all this through the testimony. You're dehumanized, and yellow people are not even human. You have no regard for them, so you don't care what happens to them. And the prisoners more so than anyone else. Instances like this go on all the time. This is just one I could bring up. I don't know what happened to him once he left that operating room. When the interrogation people came in, he was still in triage. He was laying on a stretcher. He was in really bad shape. ITT is intelligence. It's translations; it's getting information from prisoners and working a little bit with civilians. But, they came in. There's a doctor present. The

112

doctor's not concerned with intelligence. They had a captain in this case, who is a Marine officer, and two ARVN, South Vietnamese intelligence people, one of which was an officer, one of which was a staff officer, or staff sergeant. And they're the ones who interrogated him. The officer was present. He ignored the interrogation. As a matter of fact he almost went along with it. He didn't actually touch the prisoner, but he didn't say anything to stop the torture, or whatever you want to call it, that was going on.

Lt. Jon Drolshagen, 25th Infantry Division

I was a prisoner of war interrogator. I was in Vietnam from '66 to '67.

Being an interrogator the way I was, you definitely don't win hearts and minds. I've heard about these "Bell Telephone Hours," where they would crank people up with field phones. I guess we did them one better because we used a 12-volt jeep battery and you step on the gas and you crank up a lot of voltage. It was one of the normal things.

I'll give a little background. I started out in Vietnam as a platoon leader, seven months in the field doing little fire fights, killing people, etc. You get a little bit hardened, I guess. You become a super-hawk or whatever you want to put it at. After a while, people in my unit were a little bit weary of going out in the field with me. I started enjoying killing people a little bit more than you're supposed to, I guess. Even for the United States, I guess you can like it too much. I was taken out of there and put in the civic action.

The basis of the civic action is to win the hearts and minds of the people, propagandize them to our way of thinking. We're supposedly building schools for them, getting medical aid to them, food and clothing, all the nice things that you can think of that you would want to do for people that are "less than we are" so we can bring them up to our standards—which is amazing for a country that's been there an awful lot longer than we have. Instead of doing this type of thing, we had a major that enjoyed doing other types of

113

things. We worked more as an intelligence unit to gather information for our brigade and division.

My area was from the city of Tay Ninh, the Tay Ninh province, down to Phu Cuong, which Cu Chi bisected. A little bit north of that is another village that we had commandeered, some head honcho's hootch, which is a big place—you keep your beer cool in it—and where we could carry on interrogation without outside people knowing what was happening. There was another lieutenant and a major there that was an adviser to the Vietnamese battalion down there. There were Vietnamese officers, enlisted men, and NCOs and American officers, enlisted men and NCOs that were present for the wiring of prisoners. You could take the wires of a jeep battery (it's a tremendous amount of voltage), put it most any place on their body, and you're going to shock the hell out of the guy. The basic place you put it was the genitals. There were some people who really enjoyed that because people would really squirm.

The major that I worked for had a fantastic capability of staking prisoners, utilizing a knife that was extremely sharp, and sort of filleting them like a fish. You know, trying to check out how much bacon he could make of a Vietnamese body to get information. Prisoners treated this way were executed at the end because there was no way that we could take them in to any medical aide and say, "This dude fell down some steps," or something, because you just don't get them kind of cuts and things like that.

That was our basic way of getting the information that we needed from prisoners, suspects or whatever. These people were not taken in to the 25th Division headquarters, which is stationed in Cu Chi. These were utilized out in the ARVN areas. We would go back into base camp at night, and being red-blooded American like we were, we'd go down to the Officers Club and get blasted and talk to people. So I'm sure that my brigade commander, my brigade XO, and all the officers attached to headquarters and Headquarters Company, 1st Brigade, 25th Division, knew what was happening. There was no condemnation of this. People would request to go out there with us and watch it. We had pilots with us and they don't get on the ground too much. They don't see what's really happening. We would take pilots out with us to show them our side of the war, as it were. You become very hardened after being out in the field, losing a lot of people, killing a lot of people, and when you come in, torturing really is just another way of going over it.

SP/5 Don Dzagulones, Americal Division

I was an interrogator also. I was inducted into the Army in December 1967. I spent 1969 in Vietnam. I was attached to a Military Intelligence Detachment, which was attached to the Americal Division, and it was subdivided further into teams. I was with the team that was with the 11th Brigade of the Americal Division located in southern Quang Nai province.

Field phone interrogations were commonplace. I did it. I was caught. I guess you're supposed to be put in jail for it, something like two years in jail. I received a letter of reprimand and the only reason I was caught was because the man upon whom I applied the field phone was alleged to be a highly placed Viet Cong official whose mission was to infiltrate the government of Quang Nai province. His uncle was in the provincial government and after we had gotten through with the prisoner, I guess he told his uncle and his uncle raised hell. So they conducted an investigation into it.

When I used a field phone on this prisoner, I was instructed to do so by a major. We found out that the man had a lot of information and I was instructed to use any means within my abilities to get the information out of the guy. This came from an S-2 who was a major. The instructions were relayed to me after a period of let's say an hour, in which time I'm sure he conferred with the brigade commander because the guy was a real important prisoner. I'm sure he, himself, didn't originate the idea of using any tactics within my means.

I worked on that prisoner, that particular prisoner, for three days. During the three days of interrogation, MPs were

115

present at all interrogation sessions, which is a rule in Vietnam. All interrogations are conducted in the presence of MPs, who are to make sure that we adhere to the Geneva Conventions. But as it is, the MPs were usually the most sadistic people. As far as the field phone itself, I watched as the MPs applied the torture themselves. Like I didn't have to do it. They did it for me. And that night, the night of the first interrogation, a medic came to my area with a syringe with seven cc's—I believe it was of sodium pentathol—and it was kind of like an anonymous gift. I was told how to use it and it was left to my discretion whether or not I wanted to. I didn't because I was afraid of killing the guy. I didn't know too much about that particular drug.

There were numerous incidents I feel I should explain what our function was as an interrogator. Most of the prisoners were women, children, and old men. It wasn't often that we got a military-aged male and our primary function was to find something that these people had done wrong. In that part of Vietnam—I guess they call it disputed, but it's controlled by the Viet Cong; there's no doubt about it. No one ventures out anywhere at night and the Viet Cong force people to join organizations. The Viet Cong tax them heavily and these people are forced to join various organizations, each of which has a separate function in aiding the Viet Cong. So anyone that we got as a detainee prisoner who admitted to being in an organization was classified as a civil defendant, which meant that he or she went to the National Police and the National Police applied further interrogation techniques. The National Police were probably, well, they could put the Gestapo or the SS to shame. In our particular district, the favorite tactic used by the National Police was to string a guy up from a beam or a rafter or anything that would extend his hands out, get a speedometer cable, I believe it was, and kind of whip the person until either he died or talked or was unconscious. A lot of the interrogations were witnessed by officers. As I said, all of the interrogations were witnessed by MPs, none of whom ever did anything to prevent brutality.

When I first got into Vietnam, I was an observer at most interrogations for a couple of weeks just to learn what was

116

going on and how to conduct the interrogations. One of the first interrogations I witnessed took place in a hospital in which a North Vietnamese prisoner was brought in wounded. He was severely wounded. He was going into shock from loss of blood. They had gotten the prisoner at an ambush. We had an interrogation team there that was interrogating the guy, but he wasn't offering information fast enough. The brigade S-2, which is the brigade intelligence officer, a major, was there and he was dissatisfied with the proceedings so he took over the interrogation himself. He got smelling salts, hands full of smelling salts, and he held them to the guy's face to keep him conscious, to make him talk. That didn't work very well, so he poked around in the wounds and what not. And there were MPs present again.

There was a captain who was a doctor present and two or three interrogators who could easily corroborate what I'm saying. Anything I say can be corroborated. I can get people to corroborate what I say. No one took any steps to prevent the abuse of the prisoner. As I said, he was severely wounded and he was there for maybe half an hour. They were working on getting a helicopter to Medivac him up to Division for more intensive treatment, medical treatment that is.

Field phones and beatings were commonplace occurrences. As an interrogator, I was subject to the Geneva Conventions and I was watched by MPs during the interrogations. However, there were other people in our unit who were counter-intelligence, and during their interrogations there was no one ever present. They conducted their interrogations on their own. There was no one to supervise, and consequently, they took advantage of it. They always used the field phone. They never bothered to ask the person questions. One of the incidents that I know of personally, which I witnessed, was a guy who was supposed to be a spy. They'd interrogated him for about four or five hours and they alternated between beating him and wiring him up with the field phone. Subsequent to the interrogation, the guy was unconscious. I don't know if he was alive or not. They loaded him in a jeep, left the base camp, dumped him off Highway 1 somewhere off the side of the road and came back. No one ever found out

117

about the conduct of the counter-intelligence people. Another time they brought in a woman prisoner who also was alleged to be a spy. They continued the interrogation in a bunker and she wouldn't talk. I don't think she even gave them her name. So they stripped off her clothing, and they threatened to rape her, which had no effect on her at all. She was very stoic. She just stood there and looked at them defiantly. So they threatened to burn her pubic hairs, and I guess it wasn't done on purpose, I'm sure of that, but they lighted a cigarette lighter and she caught on fire. She went into shock. I guess she was unconscious, so they called the medics. The medics came and they gave the medics instructions to take her to the hospital under the pretext of being in a coma from malaria, which they did. And nothing was ever done about that.

I also had experience with Psy-Ops teams, which is basically the same thing Jon was. They were to win the hearts and minds of the people. There was one sergeant in particular who had a reputation for being a sadist. His mission was to go into areas and propagandize the people, try to win their hearts and minds over to the South Vietnamese government's side, which is an impossibility. There was no part of his mission which involved detaining people, but at least once or twice a month, he'd send in a bunch of prisoners. Usually they were old women, and, invariably, all had been beaten. One time in particular, we had five elderly ladies sent in, all of whom were beaten. One had a broken leg, I believe, and another had a skull fracture. We sent them over to the hospital for medical attention and we brought it to the attention of the people at Brigade (the majors, the captains, and the colonels). We told them that it wasn't an isolated incident, that it happened before with the same guy, but no one took any action to prevent it or to reprimand him or to see that it never happened again. As I said, it was commonplace to beat people. There were many assorted techniques used. The field phone was the most popular, though. I'm sure there's a lot more I could relate but right now I'm too nervous to think of them.

One of the favorite methods used in coercing a prisoner

118

to talk was dehydration. Our main objective in getting a prisoner to talk was to make sure we left no marks, nothing that was traceable. So the MPs were very cooperative with us. We'd get a prisoner and we'd keep him on a diet of crackers and peanut butter, which comes in C-rations. The prisoner was kept out in the sun for three or four days eating crackers and peanut butter and occasionally they'd make him do a little physical labor. If the guy wasn't suffering enough, they'd make him fill sand bags and carry them around. They did this until it was obvious that the prisoner wasn't going to talk, or the prisoner broke. No steps were ever taken to prevent these actions. There was no supervision. If people did find out about it, they just let it go, because it was an accepted practice; it was common. They were after the information and since the Vietnamese, as has been mentioned, were treated and held as less than human, anything that we did was perfectly all right.

I was trained at Fort Meade, Maryland, and officially we weren't trained to use any kind of torture tactics. A class was supposed to last for an hour. They'd lecture us for half an hour and then they'd turn the class over to Vietnam veterans, people who had been interrogators in Vietnam. It was up to them to tell us what they felt was essential to help us function as interrogators in Vietnam. Invariably the instruction would turn to various methods that they'd seen or heard of or used in torturing people in Vietnam and there are many, many, many methods.

Most of the prisoners we had were women. It wasn't uncommon to have a mother and daughter coming in the same group of prisoners. I don't know why, I can't understand it, but we had a rarity in our unit. We had a black interrogator, which is really uncommon. There aren't too many black people in military intelligence. So we found out that by threatening a woman with having the black interrogator rape her, would usually make them talk. So they'd have the woman and her daughter brought in at the same time. We'd send the daughter into a bunker and tell the mother that we were going to send the black interrogator in to rape the daughter if she didn't cooperate and give us information.

119

Usually they took it only as a threat. There were occasions on which the guy did go into the bunker, but he was a pacifist, he never did anything.

SP/5 Nathan Hale, Americal Division

I'm 24 years old. I'm a resident of Coatesville, Pennsylvania. I'm currently a student and a candle maker. I joined the Army in April of '66. My rank at discharge was Specialist 5. I was an interrogator-linguist with Americal Division.

I arrived in Vietnam in December of '67. In January of '68 I was assigned to the 1st of the 1st Cav, Americal Division. I arrived at the base camp of the 1st of the 1st Cav which is Hill 29. When I arrived there my S-2, a captain, told me that my job was to elicit information. This meant that I could elicit information in any means possible. He told me that I could use any technique I could think of and the idea is "Don't get caught," and what he meant was I could beat these people, I could cut 'em, I could probably shoot 'em—I never shot anyone—but I could use any means possible to get information—just don't beat them in the presence of a non-unit member or person. That's someone like a visiting officer or perhaps the Red Cross. And I personally used clubs, rifle butts, pistols, knives, and this was always done at Hill 29. And in the field it even gets better.

The important point here is that everything I did was always monitored. An interrogator is always monitored. I was monitored by an MP sergeant at Hill 29 who often helped me in my interrogations—he and his squad. One other incident on Hill 29—there was a man who was kicked to death by the ARVNs, the South Vietnamese. They called me the next morning and they said you have a dead prisoner. So I had to take a doctor over to confirm that he was dead. My S-2, instead of going through the necessary paper work, had him put in two 500 pound rice sacks and the troops took him out that day and dumped him. He was added to the previous day's body count. I guess that's about it. I can tell you that Americal Division has the ideal interrogation location. There

120

are MPs on the hill watching you but this doesn't mean you can't kick prisoners under the table. We used to take knives into the interrogation huts and use the guys' hands as a means of terror. I might also add that I learned everything I know from the South Vietnamese and from my Americal cohorts.

V. PRISONERS OF WAR AND REFUGEES

S/Sgt. George Smith, 5th Special Forces

I was 17 when I joined the Army. I now work for the Post Office in New Cumberland, West Virginia, and I go to Kent State University in Ohio. I was a member of the Special Forces Aide Team in South Vietnam in 1963. My camp was overrun. I was captured by the NLF troops and held prisoner for two years and released in November 1965.

We were at a camp called Hiep Hoa; it was about 30 miles out of Saigon in the Delta area. We were in one of those isolated Special Forces camps but we had a strike force of South Vietnamese that were on our payroll, and about midnight on November 23rd I was awakened by an explosion and mortar shells were falling on our house. The camp was very quickly overrun by a large NLF force, and I was captured along with three other Americans.

During the excitement of battle, of course, they were a little rougher than they were later on, but they didn't mistreat us terribly bad at the time, and I was sure that we were going to be shot, because all the stories that I had heard at Fort Bragg and after coming into Vietnam was that they didn't take prisoners, and if they did, that they tortured and eventually killed them, if not immediately.

Moderator: Were you with the other three prisoners at this time?

Smith: I was by myself when I was captured, but I was later taken behind the latrine in the camp where I met Sgt. Camacho, who was one of the mortar operators, and a string was attached to us sort of like a leash, and I thought that we had been taken behind the latrine, of course, to be shot. They set us down in a cross position but nothing happened to us at this time.

After they had rounded up all the equipment, the ammunition, weapons in the camp, they took us out over the barbed wire apron surrounding the camp, through Madame

122

Nhu's sugar cane field that we were guarding, to a small village on the Oriental River. I thought they were taking us to another place to execute us. And I was worrying about that, along with the air strike that we were under by that time. The South Vietnamese Air Force was attacking the cane field and burned down a lot of sugar cane. I thought they might accidentally drop something on us. But other than that there was no immediate fear, 'cause the guards seemed to have relaxed once we left the camp.

When we arrived in the village, everybody sat down, lit up a cigarette, offered us one, gave us some bananas to eat, patted us, and reassured us that everything was going to be all right. That they had no intentions toward us. After they took their, sort of their break after the battle, we crossed the river and went farther into the Delta area. We traveled for about three or four days until we finally reached a place where we met up with Rohrback and McClure, who were also at our camp and had been captured. This was the first we had seen of them. After we met, the four of us were taken in those little boats that they have through the canal system down into what is probably the Plain of Reeds, the swamp region, and we stayed on a little island there. They constructed a small shack just big enough for the four of us; they slept out in hammocks in the water. And they allowed McClure's foot wound to heal so he would be able to travel at a later time. They provided immediate attention for him when he was captured. He told me that they dressed his wounds the best they could. He had a fragmentation wound of the foot, which was extremely painful for him it turned out.

In the swamp then they had time to do things and they got a medic from someplace and he was quite a good medic; he was well trained; he had penicillin; he had the instruments to probe the foot and find if there were any foreign objects in it. Soon McClure's foot did heal quickly enough that we were able to move out in about ten days, I think.

We went on a long march that led generally north or northwest, I would guess, because we passed by the Tay Ninh mountain and went into the heavy jungle area. It was a long walk and very difficult for us because we didn't have shoes,

123

three of us. It wasn't because they had taken our shoes—they did try to give us some shoes, but unfortunately the Vietnamese have small feet compared with Americans, and they just didn't fit.

We carried only the things that were necessary for our existence, our hammocks and a change of clothes. And they carried all the food, and the weapons—and those big weapons they were carrying were some of the ones that we wouldn't carry because they were too heavy, like the BAR rifle that weighs 20 pounds fully loaded. They were carrying those plus sacks of rice around their neck which can weigh 10 to 15 pounds, all of their equipment, and some of our stuff that we weren't able to carry.

Moderator: Were you bound and gagged?

Smith: Never at any time was I gagged; I did, as I mentioned earlier, have a rope around my wrist, that they sort of held on to me so that if I would decide to run away that they could pull me back a little bit.

Moderator: Were you ever interrogated in this swamp?

Smith: They asked us what our names were, that was the only thing they asked us. Finally, I was interrogated after about three months.

Moderator: What type of military information were they looking for?

Smith: Well, he told us that he certainly wasn't interested in any military information that we had, because it would be outdated anyway, and he reminded me that their intelligence was far superior to any information that we might have. He wanted to present the views of the National Liberation Front, concerning the war in South Vietnam. In other words, tell their side of the story. And he asked me if I would think about it, and try to rationalize whether we were right or they were right, and to come back later and talk with him about it, and try to have a discussion about South Vietnam. We sat at tables, approximately like this, except that it was handmade in the jungle, and they served tea and sugar cubes if they had it.

Moderator: How long would a session last?

Smith: Usually an hour or so, and they gave us cigarettes

124

while we were in interrogation, and gave us a pack to take back to our hammock with us—or the bed, as the case may be.

Moderator: At any time—you were a prisoner for two years—at any time were you ever physically abused?

Smith: Never physically abused. I was really surprised to find that out, because contrary to everything we'd heard, they never once laid a hand on me; except when I was captured they pushed me around a little bit, which I would expect to do myself if I captured somebody.

Moderator: But still and all, you were a prisoner of war. There must have been difficult times. What was the attitude of the guards towards you and the other three prisoners?

Smith: Their attitudes varied from time to time. They could be very friendly, and at times they would appear very hostile towards us. We learned during our stay with them that these were reflections of political activities in Saigon, that when an NLF soldier was executed in Saigon it usually influenced their attitude to a certain extent. But it seemed that there was enough control from their commanders that they never took any hostilities out on a prisoner. They may have disliked us intensely because of what was happening, but they still were under the control of the commanders. We were told at one time that our men would like to kill you, but we have discipline and we don't allow them to do so. And I can understand that because of the things that we were doing to them in '63.

They let us listen to Radio Hanoi; they brought the radio around every evening. Of course they didn't force us to listen to it, they turned it on, and if we wanted to talk that was all right. But Radio Hanoi was warning the United States and the Saigon regime that executions had been taking place (we had heard about them), and they were warning the United States if any more executions took place (I think there were three prisoners being threatened at the time), they would definitely retaliate. They said the United States must bear the responsibility for these executions, and so this sort of put us in a crimp, because, you know, who are they going to execute besides American prisoners of war if they want to retaliate against the United States? It worried us a great deal.

125

After they had warned for probably a week that the executions would take place, I heard that the executions did in fact take place. At about that time one of the members that was captured with me, a Sergeant Rhorbach, was taken from our camp area. And it was later found out that they had reported that they had executed him; the strange thing is that they never told us that they had executed Rhorbach; they never used it for coercion. As far as we knew, he had disappeared from the earth and his name was never mentioned again.

Moderator: For the record, there was another man executed at that same time?

Smith: Yes, well this was like a final warning. They had warned some months before when they executed somebody in Saigon that had tried to blow up McNamara, but wasn't successful. But they executed him for the attempt. They had warned at that time that they were going to retaliate, but as far as I know, they didn't retaliate at that time.

Moderator: How did it make you feel? I mean you were there as a prisoner and the warnings are going out and these executions are still going on?

Smith: It's kind of a panicky situation, really, you know, that there's nothing you can do about; you know that the United States is so stubborn and bullheaded that they won't listen to someone like the NLF because they don't recognize that they exist. So how could they listen to them protesting? So, really, we were in a bad position, almost hopeless, because we knew that the United States wouldn't listen to them, and they were saying that they would retaliate, which I didn't appreciate, but gee, they were certainly within their rights. If their soldiers were being executed, there was no reason why they shouldn't retaliate.

Moderator: You were a prisoner for two years under some rather strange circumstances in the jungle. How would you describe the food that you had in terms of whether it was sufficient, adequate, whatever?

Smith: I usually had more food than I could eat; I usually ate better than they did. They brought in things like sardines for us, which they didn't eat themselves. They brought in cases and cases of sardines. And it sort of worked in a cycle, like I would be able to eat the food for a certain

126

period of time and then I would build up an intolerance toward it and I would become ill, and wouldn't be able to eat the food for a while.

As I said they gave us sardines and they brought in canned milk for us. It wasn't limited to that. On Christmas, our first Christmas, they brought in a woman who spoke English and asked us what we would like to order for Christmas dinner. We told her, well, a chicken would probably be good, with some bread, and of course this was an asinine request as far as we were concerned. But sure enough, they brought a chicken and bread, along with a paper star with a candle in it, so I had it hung in the cell for us.

Moderator: And when you say cell, uh . . .

Smith: It was like a little house, it was made of poles that they had cut nearby, in the forest there.

Moderator: When you say "bread," they had bread in the camp?

Smith: No, they told us that they did not eat bread, and they didn't even buy bread, but since we requested it, they sent men to wherever the nearest bread factory was, and got us some bread. It was at least two days away, I'm sure of that, because there were certainly no towns large enough to have a bakery, and when the bread came, it was long loaves of French bread, so it definitely wasn't made in some jungle.

We always had the biggest share of tobacco. They brought us so much one time we didn't know what to do with it. We had to store it all over the house trying to keep it from being soaked up with water from the rainy season. But the guards would run out of tobacco very soon after we got our supply because they seemed to get just a handful. They would occasionally bum a cigarette from us. They'd come up and ask us if they could have it; they never took the liberty to take our tobacco away from us.

Moderator: Did you ever receive mail? As a prisoner?

Smith: Yes, I think I received about four letters, three or four letters, anyway, while I was a prisoner, from my mother. They allowed me to write as often as I wanted to. I didn't write often because I didn't believe that the letters would be delivered if I wrote, and possibly they might use it against me

127

at some time or another. I wrote two letters, I believe, two solid letters. But they asked me and said, "You may write every week. We'll furnish you with the paper and material which is necessary to write." But I normally declined. McClure wrote a number of letters himself. How many were delivered, I don't know. The ones I did write were finally delivered to my mother.

Moderator: How would you describe the attitude of the prisoners towards your captors?

Smith: Well, I can speak for myself. I was extremely hostile and very arrogant with them. This ethnocentrism thing was strong enough that even though I was a prisoner I still looked down upon them. And how they were able to tolerate my attitude for a year or so until I finally decided that these were people, and I could look upon them as such, I don't know. But I was really a bad prisoner, and they told me at one time that I was the worst prisoner they had.

Moderator: But despite that, you were never physically abused.

Smith: Never physically abused; and finally released, which was the most unusual thing.

Moderator: Did you ever make any statements while you were a prisoner?

Smith: Yes, I made statements. Like I was telling you, these classes that we had where they presented their views and we would go back and discuss them at some length. I stated that I believed that they were basically right about Vietnam—that I didn't have any business there, that the war in Vietnam was wrong, that we were violating the Geneva agreement, that I certainly didn't want any part of it, and that all the troops should be withdrawn. This was basically what I said. We, of course, elaborated on different points of it. But these are statements I made, and I wrote a letter to that effect in one of the letters to my mother, describing the situation there and how I now felt about it, according to what I had observed from that frame of reference.

When I first came back, I was not positive that I was taking the right position, so I did considerable research on my

128

own to find out just where I was. The more research I did the more entrenched I became in my beliefs. And now I feel very strongly that what I said then was right. In fact, I say even more then than I do—even more now than I did then, and I'm not under the duress of being a prisoner of war.

Moderator: Did any of the other prisoners make statements while they were there?

Smith: All of the prisoners as far as I know made statements very similar to mine and McClure made more statements than I did, I believe, because he wrote more letters to his wife than I did. But everybody that was there was making the same statements because we got together and talked about it after the interrogation. We all generally agreed that it was a bad situation, we really didn't belong there, and that we would just be glad if the war ended and we all went home.

Moderator: It's a matter of public record that in 1965 Sergeant Comacho, Isaac Comacho, escaped from the same camp that George was at, thereby becoming the first prisoner of war to successfully escape since the Second World War. At the time that he did escape, as it appeared in *Life* magazine, Comacho made the statement that what made it possible for him to escape was the fact that George Smith was the one that covered for him. What was the net result for Comacho after he got back?

Smith: I found out after I got back that Comacho had been returned to the United States, to his home in El Paso, and that President Johnson made a special trip to El Paso to personally decorate Comacho with a Silver Star for escaping.

Moderator: In November 1965, you were finally released. Did they ever tell you why you were being released?

Smith: Yeah, the NLF told me that I was being released in direct response to the peace movement in the United States, and more specifically to replace Norman Morrison and a woman who had immolated themselves, Norman Morrison in front of the Pentagon at that time, I believe. They stated that they realized that the American people were basically peace-loving people and did not condone the actions that the United States Government was taking in South Vietnam, so they were returning two of their sons to them for the replace-

129

ment of the two who had given their lives for the cause of peace in Vietnam.

Moderator: Where were you actually first released?

Smith: I was turned over to the Australians in Pnom Penh, Cambodia.

Moderator: And when did they tell you this, about the peace movement and so on?

Smith: Well, they had mentioned the peace movement back at the camp before I was actually taken to Pnom Penh. And at Pnom Penh of course they set up a press conference for us. International reporters were there. And someone asked me a question of what I intended to do when I got back to the United States. I told him that I was going to tell the true story of Vietnam as I could see it, from my experiences. That the United States had no business in Vietnam, that it wasn't in the best interest of the American people, and that therefore we should all get out immediately. And someone asked me, "How do you intend to tell this story?" I said, "I'll probably get in touch with the peace movement when I get back because I understand they're saying similar things."

Moderator: So, did you look up the peace movement?

Smith: No, I never did.

Moderator: Why?

Smith: I ended up in Okinawa, which is a United States military base; no one has access there unless the United States military allows them to go there. I was supposed to be sent directly home, but for some reason or other they saw fit to take me to Okinawa, where they held me incommunicado, censored my mail for about five and a half months, I think it was.

Moderator: In other words, you were a prisoner again.

Smith: Yes, a prisoner of the United States Army this time. I had an escort everywhere I went, and was not allowed to do anything on my own unless I checked with the escort. I was taken to a debriefing—supposedly a debriefing—in Okinawa, which lasted about 21 days and consisted of 51 typewritten pages. And after the debriefing was almost over, before they had actually concluded the debriefing, an officer came in and informed me that I was suspected of violation of Article 104 of the UCMJ, specifically, aiding the enemy, and also suspected of misconduct in the face of the enemy. Both of these charges carry the death penalty.

Moderator: Now, if I can get this straight. Sergeant Comacho, who made the same statements, and who escaped with your assistance, was given the Silver Star?

Smith: Right, exactly.

Moderator: And you are now under court-martial charges which hold the ultimate penalty of death.

Smith: Seems rather curious.

Moderator: Yes. Would you comment on that?

Smith: Well, I suspect the fact that I opened my mouth and said I was going to look up the peace movement when I got home didn't set very well with Special Forces and the Army. And to be able to stop me from doing this, they brought the charges against me, which allowed them to hold me on Okinawa indefinitely, until maybe the peace movement forgot about me or I forgot about the peace movement.

Moderator: Before you were released, you had to sign a piece of paper relating to classified information, and they specified certain information you were not to discuss.

Smith: Right.

Moderator: Would you give us a couple of examples, a couple of things you weren't supposed to discuss?

Smith: Well, one of the strangest things—this was a secret you know; I'm under violation of the National Security Act if I discuss this thing, so I expect to be arrested as soon as I finish saying this—but I wasn't allowed to tell anybody that I received a Red Cross parcel while I was a prisoner of war.

Moderator: You did receive a Red Cross parcel back in the jungle?

Smith: Oh yes, yes we received—Comacho, McClure, and myself each received a large Red Cross parcel, probably weighed fifteen pounds apiece. They had to carry it maybe fifty miles at least because they certainly didn't have any roads in the jungle.

131

Dr. Marjorie Nelson

I'm not a veteran. I was in Vietnam from October of 1967 until October 1969. I was captured in the Tet Offensive of 1968 in Hue. I had gone to Quang Ngai in October of '67 and I had been there for four months when the Tet holiday was coming up.

I was working with a project that was basically three things. It was a day care center for refugee children, and a rehabilitation center for civilians, primarily war-injured, though we had other cases. The third thing that I was doing was, once or twice a week I was going to the local civilian prison, that is, the provincial prison, where I was examining sick prisoners.

I went to Hue for Tet to visit friends, and, of course, you know, Hue was overrun and held for some time by NLF and NVA forces. I was staying with a friend, Sandra Johnson, who was working for International Voluntary Service teaching English in Dong Thaien High School, which is a girls' high school in Hue, and she and I spent the first four days of the attack in an improvised bomb shelter in her dining room while the fighting went on outside. On the fourth afternoon, NLF soldiers came to the house and pounded on the front door. We were too frightened to respond, so they went around to the kitchen door and broke in through the kitchen. We could hear them kind of rummaging around the kitchen, and then they came to the door between the dining room and the kitchen, which was bolted from our side by two bolts, and they began to shoot the bolts off the door.

I said to Sandy, "I'm going to talk to them." And so I asked them in Vietnamese, "What do you want?" and they said, "Open the door," so we did. There were five of them. They came in, asked just a few questions—asked us if we had any weapons in the house, to which we replied, "No," and then they searched the house. We talked a bit more; they attempted to reassure us that we should not be afraid and that they did not intend to take anything. Then the fighting sort of began again and we moved out of the living room and

132

just about that time I heard something coming. I don't know what it was, but I jumped back into the bomb shelter and whatever it was hit the living room where we'd just been, and demolished the living room. So they went back outside and left us alone for two more days. Then, on the sixth afternoon, they came back and told us that we should go with them.

We were in Hue about three more days before we were officially registered as prisoners of war. We had to fill out forms in triplicate, giving our passport number, our name, who we worked for, etc. And then, finally, someone who spoke English—for the first time we met someone who spoke English—he told us that because of the continued heavy fighting in the city they couldn't keep us safely; that we were going to be taken to the mountains to study, and that when there was peace, we'd be returned to our families. So we expected to be there for the duration of the war.

That night we left with about 15 or 20 Vietnamese prisoners. We walked into the mountains and were held then in the mountains for a little over six weeks before we were released.

Moderator: Now, once you were in the mountain camp there, and even before, could you say whether there was any physical molestation of you, any abuses taken of you as a woman or as a person?

Nelson: No. This is a question that I know comes up in the minds of, well, certainly of any GI who's been in Vietnam, and many other people. Certainly this thing could have occurred, and I think on a couple of occasions, we were simply lucky that it didn't. However, once we were in the camp, it was quite clear that the cadre also were concerned about this, and they made sure that our privacy was respected. In the first camp we were living with a Vietnamese family, and we were living family style—I mean we didn't have a separate room. And then in the second camp, we had our own house.

At the second camp Sandy and I—that is, my girlfriend and I—were the only ones there during the whole time. When we were separated from the main group of American prisoners, two fellows came with us. They stayed a couple of days and then went on.

Moderator: And in the first camp, you were with how many other people?

Nelson: We were with about 15 or 20 Vietnamese prisoners, and when we got there we found about 25 American men already there, all of whom had been captured in Hue.

I didn't see any Vietnamese prisoners mistreated. I talked with all the American men. None of them had been threatened or mistreated, except that at the time of capture, I mean when they were captured, several of them had their shoes or watches or rings taken away from them. One man said that he had been—and I think I quote exactly, "They made me walk over barbed wire on the way out." He did not indicate whether he thought that was a deliberate act or simply an order to go that way and he went.

This was during a battle, when he was captured. I think two or three others had received wounds before they were captured, you know, fragments and that sort of thing. They received medical attention and a nurse came two or three times a week to dress their wounds, which was adequate except for two of them: that was the man I mentioned, whose feet were in bad shape, and another man who'd taken a big piece of something in his side; they needed more medical attention. I spoke to the camp commanders in the best Vietnamese that I could about this. I said that I felt they needed more medical care and they should be sent to a hospital, if possible. He seemed very uncomfortable with this. He said, "I'm sorry. We'll do the best we can. The situation is temporarily very difficult for us, but please don't worry. I'll do the best that I can for these men."

I didn't need any medical attention at that camp except for blisters, which I could take care of myself. But about two weeks later, at the second camp, I came down with amoebic dysentery, and the cadre, I call him—that is, the man who spoke English and who was in charge of prisoners—immediately had a nurse come and see me. She gave me a standard antidiarrhea treatment, which didn't help very much. And so, after about a day and a half, when it was apparent to them that I was really quite ill, I heard them talking about trying to get me a doctor. So I waited all that day and all the next day and finally, just before supper time on the second day, a doctor did arrive, a young man who'd been educated in Hanoi at medical school, very well trained. He examined me and prescribed appropriate therapy. Any of you who know medicine, he gave me chloromycetin, and I was really surprised, because I expected at best that I'd get tetracycline; but he did have chloromycetin. He also gave me fluids, intravenous fluids, by dermoclysis, and in four days my symptoms were gone.

Moderator: After you were released from prison by the Viet Cong, did you stay in Vietnam?

Nelson: No, I returned to the United States for about four months, and then I went back.

Moderator: And what was your job when you returned to Vietnam?

Nelson: I returned to the project in Quang Ngai that I was working with before.

Mrs. Virginia Warner

I am the mother of James Warner, who has been a prisoner in Vietnam, North Vietnam, since 1967 in October. I'm here to ask the American people to help get this thing over with.

First of all, I want to say, I am an American. I'm sure I'm going to be labeled Communist; I'm sure I'm going to be labeled revolutionary, but I am not. I am an American. I love my country. It's being torn apart by this war. I want to appeal to the middle-aged, middle-class America. We have to wake up and realize what's happening to us. My son's been a prisoner, and, of course, I'm interested in him coming back. I'd love to have him back, and I know he wants to be back, but this isn't the only consideration. We have to consider the people in Vietnam. What would we do, what would you and I do, if a Vietnamese plane flew over and bombed our town? How would we react to somebody that we've captured? I think my son isn't being humanely treated. I don't think he's been brutally treated, but he doesn't get steak; I'm sure he doesn't get chicken like George Smith got. But I think he has food enough to sustain him. Lieutenant Frischman said the food that they get is enough to sustain them, and if we can sustain him till he comes back, fine. We're allowed to send him a package every other month. We send, oh, aspirins, vitamin capsules, and such things as that.

We hadn't heard from him for two and a half years. We knew he was a prisoner. We knew he had been captured by the North Vietnamese. We began to write letters for foreign newspapers and letters to foreign governments to try to get the Vietnamese to tell us about the prisoners, where they were and who they were. Now we've gotten two lists. I don't understand why we claim the lists aren't complete; I don't understand that. Of course, maybe it's because my son's name has appeared on it and you know, in the back of my mind, maybe I'm satisfied. But I've talked to other families and the circumstances of their son's disappearance or their husband's disappearance is quite different, and it's perhaps that the North Vietnamese don't know where they are.

These are the things we have to rationalize with. We have to stop and think what's happening to our country and to that country. Is it worth going on, is it worth tearing everybody apart? I think, I don't know what else to say. I'd just like to say that since Hanoi has said that if we set a date, they'll talk about the release of the prisoners, is that asking so much, just to set a date? Let's put them on the spot. Let's put them on the spot. Let's set a date and see if they really will live up to their word. They've told the whole world that this is what they'll do, and if they're interested at all in world opinion, like we've been told they are, I think they will. I think they'll listen.

And will America listen? Will middle-aged, middle-class America listen? Don't let our country be torn apart by this.

Jim Clark, AID and Catholic Relief Services

I was in Vietnam from 1966 through 1969. I was there originally with the Agency for International Development. I resigned from that organization in 1968 and took a position with Catholic Relief Services. I coordinated a project dealing with social welfare and the training of social workers in Vietnam under that. With AID, I was a refugee officer for a year on the central coast and I spent a little over a year in Saigon as a special assistant for voluntary agencies.

When I was in Phu Yen, I was new in the country—this was back in '66. I went out to a refugee camp. The conditions were really deplorable. There were about 3000 people living on a sandspit in tin huts with rooms about eight-by-eight with seven people in each room. There was a reception camp with buildings that were about forty feet long, and twenty feet wide with 400 to 500 people in each—impossible as that sounds, but it was true. I went out there, and I was really depressed about the situation.

The refugee situation in Vietnam is deplorable. I'll briefly go over the reasons for the generation of refugees in Vietnam, where they're located, who the refugees are, and some of the economic implications.

I don't know what all the errors are in relation to our involvement with Vietnam, but there have been several. And I don't know how we can get out of this problem. Between 1964 and the fall of 1969, the American effort in Vietnam, directly or indirectly, produced an internal generation of refugees, which was on a level probably unknown before in the world. Twenty-five percent, to use some estimates, of the entire population of the country have been displaced. The estimates run anywhere from two million and on up. The agrarian economic base of the country has been destroyed. The cultural identity factors of the population have been severely strained. Health and welfare problems, totally beyond the experience of the Vietnamese in terms of the extended family and the nature of the people to generally solve their own problems, have been spawned. We're facing a problem now where we're going to leave. We're picking up our

137

toys and we're going home. And we're going to leave this country ravaged.

An investigation of the nature of the refugee problem and how the problem affects the economic base of the country may result in a perspective which may be beneficial in evaluating the current state of affairs. Who are the refugees? Where are the refugees from? Where are the refugees currently located? And what may we expect in terms of the refugees in the future? Traditional discussions of Vietnam generally begin with the migration of refugees from the North. In 1954 some 900,000 people did leave; some 700,000 of these people were Catholics. They had the benefits of an educational system; they had money. When they came to South Vietnam, their resettlement was not that difficult a problem. This group also, this original group, is distinguished by the fact that they, unlike the people who would become refugees later, *did* make a choice. To borrow a popular phrase among propagandists, they voted with their feet. They made a choice and came South. This cannot be said of the vast majority of the 2.5 million people who were to follow them. The refugee camps and towns in the provincial capitals today are swollen by people who once populated the rural areas of the country.

An analysis of the reasons given by the refugees themselves finds that they are divided in their reasons for leaving. The causal agents of movement differed from area to area. The degree of enemy activity and the degree of allied action in response to the activity were important determinants. The pattern which was normally adhered to was an air drop of leaflets encouraging the population in NLF-controlled areas to evacuate. However, an analysis of movement based on refugee interviews would imply that the leaflets served more to ease the conscience of allied forces engaged in future action than to actually result in refugee generation or migration.

Planning for refugee generation may have been unrealistic in expecting persons to leave their homes and livelihood and their extended families for migrations to areas of high unemployment and, in some cases, local hostility. If military leaf-

138

let dropping was unrealistic, as surveys seem to indicate, the resulting deaths and casualties raise some questions as to the morality of allied actions. The assumption that persons not leaving free fire zones were enemies also was a generalization having severe moral implications. The hostility toward refugees by urbanites went beyond urban-rural conflict. Refugees were, in many cases, the families of NLF forces, Assistance to such people was often viewed negatively by Vietnamese government personnel as aid to dependent enemy.

I had a conversation with a province chief in Phu Yen one day. He was quite blunt with me and he expressed the opinion, "Why should I help these people, who have sons and fathers out fighting in the countryside and who, if they had the opportunity, would slice my throat?" I tried to convince him, of course, at that time, that if he'd start acting like a decent human being towards these people and accepting them as people, the situation might change around.

Persons living in enemy-controlled areas could be encouraged to leave directly or indirectly. A direct movement would result from forced movement, where allied forces would be airlifted into an area, round up residents, and airlift them out. Though this was not a common method, it did occur from time to time. Notable examples would be the Iron Triangle Operation of 1967 and several efforts in the DMZ in the North. Refugees might also be encouraged to leave through heavy military bombardment or artillery. Among refugees in Vinh Long Province in the Delta, about 20 percent of all families had either experienced wounds or deaths in their families as a result of allied artillery. In Phu Yen province 18 percent listed such artillery as reasons for their becoming refugees. Direct intervention resulting in refugee movement would also include instigation of battle or conflict in densely populated areas. Eight percent of the Vinh Long refugees and four percent of the Phu Yen refugees listed family deaths, or deaths of neighbors in such battles, as reasons for their migrations. Approximately one-fourth of the refugees in Phu Yen cited ground military operations as a primary motive for their decision to move. When artillery ground operations and forced movement are added together as causal factors, the total percentage represented is 47.2 percent. Thus about half of all the refugees were generated by direct intervention of American and allied forces. This group cannot be said to have voted with their feet.

The indirect generation of refugees results from allied pressure on NLF forces to a level that causes the enemy to increase demands on the local population to a degree which becomes intolerable to some members of the population. The bombing of supply routes and the firepower brought down upon NLF and North Vietnamese forces resulted in shortages of both personnel and supplies. As tax rates and the drafting of local youth is on the upswing, the potential degree of dissatisfaction with the occupying forces will increase. In Phu Yen, about 30 percent of the refugees listed coercive activities and general hardships from VC activities as the primary cause for their decision to move. It should be acknowledged that the situation in other provinces would be different in accordance with the variables related to the degree of allied activity, religion, and the period of time that any particular faction was in control.

The second form of indirect movement would be those persons who migrated to urban areas to take advantage of specialized local economic advantages. In Phu Yen the construction of a large air base offered high-paying day labor jobs to women and older men. Persons who could only be marginally employed in rural areas found employment in areas where there were large concentrations of allied forces. Prostitution, laundry services, truck and vehicle washing services, and snack bars were primary examples of such new entrepreneur vocations. Of the Phu Yen refugees, 7.2 percent listed economic and social reasons for their reasons for movement.

The final category of movement cannot be assigned to either direct or indirect allied involvement. In hamlets and villages which were only marginally controlled by the Saigon government there occurred constant reprisals and terror against government and Vietnam officials. School teachers, health officials, and any functionary of the government was endangering himself and his family by remaining in insecure areas. Nighttime assassinations and abductions were quite common. In Phu Yen 16.5 percent of the refugees could be so classified. The reliability of this data gathered must be questioned to some degree in terms of the faction which was responsible for taking the interviews. A Hawthorne effect, or an effect of people saying what you want them to say, is obviously probably at work here. When we tried the same forms with non-refugees, as to why their neighbors had left the countryside, 95 percent gave Viet Cong action as the primary reason; 15 percent of the refugees reported threats by the Viet Cong against them if they were to seek refuge in government areas.

There are also on record several refuge hamlets which suffered from attack by the Viet Cong. The reasons for the attack were not always clear. In some cases the reasons were related to the population turning against the Viet Cong infra- structure members. In others, the Viet Cong were attempting to get farmers to resume planting and harvesting rice crops necessary to the food supply. In summary, one can assume that several variables played a contributing factor to refugee generation. Fear of either allied or Viet Cong forces are repre- sented in approximately 90 percent of the refugee popula- tion. It would appear unrealistic to view the refugees as totally committed to either of the contending factions. Their eventual reasons for migration were rooted in their concern for their personal security, not because of political ideology.

Persons who became refugees were not all located in government subsidized camps. People with relatives in the cities, with salable skills, with cash savings, often avoided the horrors of camp life and resettled themselves. Conversely, the people who lacked vocational skills, who lacked contacts in urban areas, who possessed no cash savings, and most of all, who had no wage earner in the family tended to populate the official refugee camp. The persons seeking assistance in the refugee camps (and who would eventually number close to two million persons), were those members of society who would most likely be assigned to the lowest socioeconomic realm of society.

141

If we look at a breakdown of the age groups of the people who were in these camps, we find that in the age range of 20-45, males are outnumbered by females by 50 percent. The females in the 20-24 age group are underrepresented in terms of the total population. Among children and young people, the males slightly outnumber the females. As a percentage of the total the under-21 group represents nearly 58 percent of the total population. The fact that over 50 percent of the population is under 20 could be expected from similar studies of other emerging nations. However, the population distribution may be important in terms of the future economic state of the country, and the government expectations related to future refugee conditions.

What inference can we make from the demographic makeup of the in-camp population? To begin with, we might note that the large base of children associated with the population pyramid is characteristic of rapidly expanding populations. Past population statistics seem to confirm this trend. The next growth rate of Vietnam has been estimated to be from 1-2 percent. However, considering the large number of children in refugee camps, we must assume that there is a higher birth rate amongst the refugee camps than outside. Concerning the growth of Vietnam, population-wise, it has grown rather rapidly. In 1937 the population of South Vietnam was only four and a half million people. In 1959 it was 13.8 million. And we can expect from statistical progression ratios that by 1994 the population of Vietnam will approach thirty million people.

The distribution of the sexes, combined with our knowledge of their former rural locations, seems to suggest that many of the males remained behind in the rural areas. Presumably, since these areas were controlled by the NLF, many of the persons absent from the population are probably troops with the NLF. Thus, the hostility of many government officials, particularly military officers, toward dependent enemy merits some consideration.

An occupational survey among persons in refugee camps in 1967 found 3000 persons, out of a sample of 62,000 adults, listing their occupation as soldier. If we assume that

142

approximately half are males, we can assume that one in ten males are soldiers; this would be about one-half of the national average. Therefore, the other half must be some place else. Prior to assuming that all males absent who are not represented in the population are Viet Cong, one could consider that many have been killed in prior allied engagements or artillery bombardments. Such deaths would contribute to the welfare status of in-camp refugees in that there is no wage earner in the family. The evidence at this point would seem to suggest that the missing male population is either dead, has remained behind to work the family field, has become a fighting member of the NLF, or is part of the government forces.

The rural origins of the typical refugee family create the expectation that most former refugees followed a farming vocation. This expectation was confirmed by an occupational survey administered in 1967. Nine out of ten male adults listed farming as their primary form of occupation. The survey covered 113,000 people and the results bore out the agricultural emphasis. At the same time that the occupational survey was made, persons interviewed were asked if they desired to learn a new trade. Nine out of ten said they weren't interested in doing that because they wanted to go back to the countryside. Seventy-three percent of those interviewed expressed a desire to return to their original villages. When asked when they would return, they indicated they would return when the war was over or when it was secure and safe from both of the contending factions.

Returning to the demographic data mentioned earlier, we can see that the number of family heads, traditionally the elders of the extended families, may not be fully appreciative of contrary desires by younger members of their families. That is, after you've seen Nah Trang, who wants to go back to the farm? With over 50 percent of the members being young persons, there is reason to believe that many of the people will have no desire to return to the life of the rural areas. Many of the refugees have been away from their former homes for periods of four years or more. In October of 1965 there were over 700,000 refugees. Studies of rural-urban migration indicate a positive correlation of time in urban participation. The longer one remains in an urban area, particularly after two years, the greater one's involvement and identity with the urban structure. It is unlikely that these people will want to go back and farm the fields.

Other factors mitigating against a return of the refugee population to the farming areas are continued insecurity or future insecurity as the allied troop withdrawal continues. In that current land reform measures require that a person receiving title be farming the land, some farmers may return to find that the land they once farmed as tenants now belongs to someone else. These factors, which mitigate against the return of refugees to their homes, may be crucial to the future of the country.

The government policy towards refugees has always been one of assuming that one day the refugees will return and the problem will evaporate. If refugees do not return, or if a substantial number remain in the cities, problems of welfare and urban slums will no doubt continue. Posters have begun to appear in Vietnam and in refugee areas encouraging refugees to return to their villages. The reasons go beyond the urban problems of welfare and overcrowding. Crops are not being planted, and the country's important economic base crop, rice, is in need of labor capital. In addition, security in the countryside requires a population from the urban areas who can reasonably be expected to support the central government. The final consideration, which would appear to confirm the fact that many refugees will not be returning to their rice fields, is related to a political decision made by the United States government in 1968.

Reacting in part to increased pressures from voluntary agencies, the press, and Senator Edward Kennedy's Refugee Subcommittee, a decision was made to reclassify refugee camps, which had received all of the assistance required by law, as having been resettled into New Life hamlets. What this meant was that after receiving a cash payment, so many sacks of cement, so many sheets of roofing, and having met communal requirements related to a classroom for every hundred children and one toilet for every twenty families, the

144

refugee camps were delisted. The degree of this type of delisting of refugees can be seen in noting that in the first ten months of 1968, 168,000 refugees were resettled on location, as compared to 86,000 who were listed as having returned to their villages. The process was guaranteed to reduce the number of refugees. Unfortunately the condition of the refugee, his future, and the future of the country were not considered. It would be like if we had a welfare program in the States and we said, "Well, we'll give everyone $100 and after that we'll say that he's not welfare any more." It's just totally unrealistic. One can imagine the tragedy of this measure if similar government measures were to be incorporated into the welfare programs we have for the poor in the United States.

The actual location of the refugee camps should also be mentioned as a factor in understanding the social and economic impact of the problem. The most populated areas of the country, the area around Saigon and the Delta area, account for only 20 percent of the refugees. The northern areas of the country account for the remainder. In part, this relates to the firmer hold by the NLF and North Vietnamese units in that part of the country, and the greater intensity of fighting in the area. Unfortunately, the economic potentiality of the northern area is extremely limited. The topography of the north is mountainous and severe. And what land that is available for cultivation is highly prized. As the refugees flooded into the secure provincial capitals it became impossible to employ them or to assist them by providing land on which they might farm. In the majority of cases the refugees were placed upon barren, uncultivatable land. To return to the free fire zones was impossible, and employment locally was equally impossible. Unemployment rose from a level of .8 percent before migration began to a postmigration level of 33.4 percent.

Only 2 percent of the refugees from Phu Yen province continued to earn an income from farming. Among those who were able to find employment, many were forced to accept wages substantially lower than they earned before becoming refugees. In Phu Yen, income levels averaged 50 percent lower than premigration income levels, the average wage being about thirty cents a day. Thus, the location of refugees was a primary factor leading to high unemployment.

Summing up our knowledge of the refugee family, our profile would suggest that the average refugee is a farmer who sought refuge from indirect or direct allied action and is not stressing a political preference when he migrates. When he arrives in the secure area he will not be able to farm; will face some political hostility; will probably be a child, an old person, or a female; be unemployed, or marginally employed. In addition, the period he will remain in a refugee camp will be an extended one, greater than two years. His chances of being administratively resettled are greater than his chances of returning home. The true economic impact of the refugee problem has not yet been felt in Vietnam. The reason for this is because great volumes of United States dollar-support of the government of Vietnam—in a wartime private or indirect support factor, related to United States military factor, related to United States military expenditures and construction and services to well-paid allied forces—is in effect.

The prewar economy of Vietnam was, like many Asian countries, a two-crop agrarian economy. There were other exports, including some tea. But rubber production from French rubber plantations, and rice production from the Mekong Delta were predominant. The effects of the war on South Vietnam's exports cannot be minimized. In 1961, South Vietnam's exports were valued at $76 million. By 1964 the exports values were down to $48 million. In '65, again down to $35 million. In '66 down to $20 million. In 1967 a brief increase in exports took place, but was followed by a further decline in exports in '68. Rice became an import in 1965. Where South Vietnam had exported $33 million worth of rice in 1964, it imported $15 million worth in 1969. Rubber production fell from an export dollar value of $43 million in 1961 to $8 million in 1968.

As production and exports fell, the dollar deficit expanded and foreign exchange reserves fell. To function, the government of Vietnam became more dependent on the United States. In 1969, the American government was under-

146

writing, directly or indirectly, 60 percent of the South Vietnamese budget. The form that this aid to South Vietnam took was in indirect and direct aid. Direct aid was generally either food for freedom imports, or support of the costly commercial import program. The commercial import program allows Vietnamese citizens to purchase foreign goods with piasters. The piaster, being inflated by increased government issue of notes and the absence of domestic articles to buy with monies being generated by American forces, is thus made valuable. The United States Government would use dollars to purchase consumer items and sell the items to the Vietnamese government at favorable exchange rates. The government would then sell the items to the local citizens. The indirect gain offered by the United States was similar to that generated in tourist economies.

By waging a war that destroyed the normal source of export-income, the economic base was changed radically. The new export item was similar to that offered by college towns or small down-state capitals in the United States. Vietnam was dependent upon GIs spending money on the local economy. If the GIs are to be withdrawn, the economic export item would evaporate and the country would be without any base to support the economy, except monies received through direct aid. Generally, by being dependent upon GIs, as you withdraw the GI (and having done away with the rice and rubber export crops), the Vietnamese economy no longer has anything to have its roots in. And the people who once did the farming, as I pointed out earlier, cannot go back, nor can we expect them to go back and get the rice crops and the rubber crops going.

I think that when we recognize these factors, these statistics—boring as they are, do point out that the future of Vietnam is in very serious trouble. The people have been uprooted, their culture has been destroyed, the extended family has been severely broken up, we have overcrowding in the cities and tremendous slums. Saigon has grown from a city of 600,000 in 1960, to close to three million today, with people living in the streets. There is no future hope, economically, that these people are going to get back on their feet in the immediate future. I suggest that we have a very serious problem in Vietnam that we have not given consideration to.

In our rush to get out, in our desire to get out, I ask those of you who think on this to consider, when we do leave, what we are leaving behind and is there anything that we can do? Is there any way that we can get out? I don't think we know what we are doing there or we haven't proven that we have. Is there any way that we can get out and help these people? Is there anything that we can do other than leave this tragedy?

VI. "I CALL THE TIME I SPENT IN VIETNAM 'DEAD TIME.'"

Major Jon Bjornson, 8th Field Hospital

I was in Vietnam in 1964 and '65. This has been a rapidly changing five years in terms of my very close acquaintance with the war in Vietnam. I think that our attitudes have changed from advising to frustration to violence to atrocities, and now it's as if we are attempting to develop a conscience. I don't think we have developed enough of a conscience. I think that My Lai's can still take place in Vietnam, but I think because of the My Lai exposure, it's going to be less likely.

In terms of why, the whys involve a lot of things. In the first place probably the main thing is Army training. Army training is dehumanizing. The Army knows how to train soldiers, and so do the Marines, and so do the Navy. Most of you experienced basic training, and one of the things that happens in basic training is you don't get much sleep. When you become an automaton, you begin to follow orders—the idea of killing and sticking bayonets into the model soldiers, the whole business of the gooks, the Vietnamese are inferior, which is constantly drummed into your heads. It's a kind of programming. Also the Army knows that a squad of nine men is probably the most cohesive group of human beings you can get in terms of numbers. The likelihood is good that this group will support each other, will fight to save each other's lives, and that this is more important than what they're fighting for or why they're fighting or why they're there. They know this. And this is why you have a nine-man group. Most GIs in combat situations—and this goes back to the Revolutionary War—don't usually fight for a cause or for patriotism or for much else. They do acquiesce to a system, and the system tells you what to do. Because of the consequences of not doing it, you go into the military and do what they say.

149

A few other things I'm sure happened. It's a tremendous change going from an affluent country to an extremely poor country like any country in Southeast Asia. I think we have some sense of guilt. There's a tremendous kind of racist unconscious that I guess we all have, and again this is programmed; it's reinforced. The Vietnamese are inferior, and this has been mentioned many times. And it's also a kind of a strange attraction. As I'm sure you know, many occidentals become very attracted to the Orient and stay there. I'm sure many of the vets here have been involved with Vietnamese girls. So, it was one thing one day to call a Vietnamese soldier a gook, and that night to sleep with a Vietnamese girl. We did it. That causes a lot of ambiguity, a lot of confusion in one's mind.

Furthermore—and applicable to any war—the whole concept sort of licenses what we would call psychological regression. It licenses us to act out our impulses. We all have a certain sense of sadism, and this licenses violence. You've got a programmed soldier in combat with a gun and then you've got a hierarchy in the military. When I was in Vietnam, the generals and the colonels would say, "If we can only get some American soldiers here, they would react. The Vietnamese, these ARVN, they just won't fight." Well, the Vietnamese are very patient. You can't hustle the East. We got our own troops there because the generals wanted it. But the generals were wrong, as we all know.

It's beginning to look like we don't want to fight any more than the ARVN. So, I would say, probably the main thing is the training. When you say to a man, as we said in the Nuremberg trials, that the defense of obeying an order isn't good enough, I would question this. The American GI has a great deal of difficulty disobeying an order after the kind of training he goes through.

SP/4, Donald Donner, 86th Combat Engineers

I'm from Fayetteville, Arkansas. I served with the 86th Engineers from approximately September '67 to July of '68.

150

I'm an OCS dropout. I decided I couldn't stand the extra year. It was a hard decision there at the last.

It wasn't till OCS that I started realizing some of the things that were being done to me. One of the things that we found out after we had been in OCS for a while was that there was a purpose for all the Mickey Mouse harassment which we were put under. We were put under immense physical strain, running several miles, several tens of miles each day. We were put under what is for the Army, at least, the intense mental strain, the studies there, but they weren't that tough. We were put under intense emotional strain, being away from everybody, being not allowed to leave the barracks for about five months. And we were told later that the purpose of this was sort of a Pavlov's dog type thing. That after a person is put under immense strain for a long period of time that he sooner or later snaps. After that snap occurs, he becomes much more receptive to any ideas which are given him, and that was the entire purpose of all the harassment.

Well, I started looking back and putting that together with AIT and basic. The same forces were operating there. They shave your head. They make you lose your entire sense of identity. Instead of reacting as the individual, you are reacting as a group. The group, honorary eliteness—that's not quite the word, but it's forced upon you. You must react together or you're all punished. This continues and continues and continues. I was lucky in the sense that when I was at OCS, Dr. Howard Levy was on trial, and Dr. Levy changed my thinking for me in a very large fashion. He at least made some of the others think. I don't know what else I can say except for that.

Lt. Scott Moore, 9th Infantry Division

I'm 26 years old; I'm from New York City. I was a 1st lieutenant in the Infantry. I was a platoon leader for five months and Forward Resupply after that. I served with the 2nd/39th, 9th Infantry Division.

151

I think it was a matter of the training I'd received when I went through Officer Candidate School at Benning and I was a Tactical Officer after that. And like, I was gung-ho and just in a weird mentality. When I think back on it, it's difficult to believe I felt like that once. But to me, at that time, there was no humanness. These people were subhuman, and well, they were—the expression is "gook." There was just this inhumane attitude in general. So usually, at least the way I saw it, nothing very much was said about it.

L/Cpl. Scott Shimabukaro, 3rd Marine Division

It's obvious that military men have the attitude that a gook is a gook, and in the United States, before men go into the military, there's a great deal of this racism directed toward the Asians in the United States. But some men manage to make it into the service with an indifferent attitude. But once they get into the military, they go through this brainwashing about the Asian people being subhuman—all the Asian people, I don't just mean the South Vietnamese. All Asian people.

I want to relate this as a personal experience that I encountered when I was in the service. Before I went into the Marine Corps, I grew up in an all-white and Chicano neighborhood, and I encountered a moderate amount of racism; it didn't bother me much. When I went into the Marine Corps, I thought I was going to serve my country and be a brave Marine and a good American. As I stepped off the bus at UCMD, San Diego, the first words that greeted me were, the DI came up to me and said, "Oh, we have a gook here today in our platoon." This kind of blew my mind because I thought I was a pretty cool guy myself. But, ever since then, all during boot camp, I was used as an example of a gook. You go to a class, and they say you'll be fighting the VC or the NVA. But then the person who is giving the class will see me and he'll say, "He looks just like that, right there." Which goes to show that the service draws no lines, you know, in their racism. It's not just against the South Vietnamese or the North Vietnamese. It's against the Asians, as a people all

152

over the world. This is proved anywhere the Americans have gone in Asia. There's been a great deal of friction between the people—the Asian people and the military as an establishment. They have subjugated the people, under this guise of the people being less than human.

Mike Nakayamo, 1st Marine Division

I was in the 1st Marine Division, 1st Battalion, 5th Marines.

I wanted to rap about racism directed against Asians in the military and in Vietnam. First of all, I felt quite a bit of racism before I joined the service; okay, that's understood. When I got into the service I experienced amplified racism. As soon as I got off the bus at my boot camp, I was referred to as Ho Chi Minh. I was referred to as Jap and gook constantly through my training. Then I knew; I was going to go overseas to fight for this country.

I can rap about quite a few instances, right in boot camp, but I'll just move on to my experiences in Vietnam. While in Vietnam, I was in the infantry, but a few times they let you come back to the rear. Most Marines are allowed to go into PXs without showing an ID, and I was not allowed to go into the PX on a number of occasions with an ID because I was yellow. I was constantly referred to as gook in Vietnam also, and relating this back to the United States, I know a number of my Asian brothers and sisters who are being referred to as gooks by returning servicemen, by American people in the Los Angeles area.

Orville Carey, 1st Logistics Command

I was in 1st Logistics Command in Pleiku. I was a postal clerk. Well, I was in administrative service for most of my time in the service. Most administrative service is about 90 percent white, maybe 10 percent black, and I originally was in Germany.

153

I volunteered to go to Vietnam to get away from what I considered overt racism that was going on over there. I probably could have stood it generally a little bit better if I had been maybe in a field company with more blacks, but it was only about four blacks in a company of about maybe 70 people, 70 or 100 people and four blacks, and it was just a little bit too much. There was no chance for a promotion. You were handed out all the vile details, and in general we got a lot of practical jokes and pranks pulled on us. The only way I could get out of Germany was to volunteer to go to Vietnam.

Upon arriving in Vietnam, I found out that the situation in the rear echelon companies is much the same. There are very few blacks in rear echelon companies, mostly whites. The excuse was, I believe, that there weren't enough blacks qualified to work in things like finance, personnel, and the other backup companies.

Pfc. William Light, Americal Division

My name is William Light. I served in the Americal Division of the 1/6, E Company, Echo Recon. I was a grunt.

I'm going to start off with racism on a personal basis. For reasons of my own, I chose not to go over to Vietnam. Behind this, I was railroaded, and handcuffed, and taken under guard to Vietnam. They forwarded orders to my company commander of my background when I was in basic and AIT, relevant to my behavior. From the jump, he discriminated against me. I was commonly referred to as a "field nigger."

I was on an operation. We were under attack by a regiment of VC. The outcome was like seven to eight guys out of about 35 left. The first thing my first sergeant did when he called in was to find out if I was dead or not. The majority of my company consists of white guys, but the majority of brothers are in the field. The ratio is like 60 to 40 and most brothers, Puerto Ricans, and Mexicans, have to walk point to more or less prove their manhood, on an individual basis, that

154

they are just as much man as the next guy. Consequently there were all forms of racism.

I was in the stockade at Lon Bin for three months. I saw a brother fed rat poison because he chose not to do some of the things that the racist MPs asked him to do. A lot of brothers were beaten, handcuffed, and gagged, and thrown into solitary confinement without food. My first meal in solitary confinement was mashed potatoes and coffee grounds. That was it. You'd be surprised at the things that happen over there. They had their ways. Whitey would play this game. He'd have us ready to go into the field before we even got over there. We were trained to go to the field back in the States—so Whitey gets the typewriter, you get the rifle. That's the way it went down. You couldn't beat the game.

There were a number of these degrading things that they did. Like a number of blacks in the rear, they had jobs assigned to them like KP, commonly referred to as shit detail. And getting trash, etc., things like that. And the viewpoint, you know, like from the eyes of the Vietnamese, like, this is the type of thing a degrading person would do. It was very few whites that had anything to do with this type of detail and like they're destroying our culture and the Vietnamese culture. Now the Vietnamese will never again regain their culture as it was. Mostly they had black guards guarding black prisoners; like, they gave them a thing, like, if he gets away you have to serve the rest of his time. More or less the black guys there were more harder than the white ones.

Lt. Barry Romo, Americal Division

If I can say one word before you go on, just one word about the Chicano, the Puerto Rican, the brown. If it's all right. Thank you. The brown people, the Puerto Rican, the Chicano, suffer from a problem in America, not only of racism, but of a language and a cultural difference. The ghettoizing that goes on in his early life, his economic background of relegation to farm work, etc., puts him in a posi-

155

tion that when he goes in the service, the only thing the service feels he's qualified for is the front line and infantry duty. As a consequence, when he gets to the field, he cannot relate to his officers or NCOs. He can't understand the language and he can't understand the culture behind it. The Chicano, the brown, the Puerto Rican suffers statistically more casualties than any other minority and the white. I think this has to be brought out and it has to be stopped.

YN3 Evan Haney, Naval Support Activity, Da Nang

I would like to point out that if you took the Vietnamese war, or the American war, as it is, and compared it to the Indian wars a hundred years ago, it would be the same thing. All the massacres were the same. Nowadays they use chemical warfare; back then they put smallpox in the blankets and gave them to the Indians. You could just go right on down the line and name them out and they would be the same thing. One thing I would like to bring up about racism is that I have grown up with it all my life, and when I was small I was exposed to this, and I kept growing and growing and learning. But it was so much that when I watched TV or something and watched the Indians and the cavalry, I would cheer for the cavalry. That's how bad it was.

Right now a lot of Indian people are . . . they're not going back to the old ways, but they're thinking about the old ways. You can take any culture of these people up here on the panel, any culture of you out there, and if you look back into it deep, they had something good. Way back, they had it. And then people started getting into a money bag, and that's when it all happened.

When we made treaties long ago, it was for as long as the grass shall grow and as long as the rivers shall flow. The way things are going now, one of these days the grass isn't going to grow . . . and the rivers aren't going to flow.

Sgt. Jim Weber, Americal Division

Prior to going into service, I was a manager of a shoe store—it's a chain across the country. I had a relatively easy job, well-paying job. And so I imagined I would be flag waver because I had a little bit of money and I wouldn't care about; you know, I had a racist attitude. Of course, we all still have racist attitudes. I, I didn't care about anyone else. You know, I cared about myself and I, I got drafted into the Army and it, it made quite a big change because I was waving flags all the time that I was on my train, you know, down to South Carolina where I got my murder training.

And I—okay, I went in there, and my complete moral worth was completely destroyed. I mean I was a worthless human being. The worst thing that you can be in the military is to be called a civilian. And so they had to completely re-socialize us, which they were very effective at doing. I didn't agree with everything, but I went along with it. Then I was sent on to advanced genocide training down at Ft. Polk, Louisiana. And this, this is where I got, you know, this is where I started to hate, hate anything that wasn't exactly like me. Anything that wasn't a fighting machine. Gooks. You've heard that mentioned here, but I don't think you really know what it means unless you know how much hate is instilled in one person, how much, how much really guilt, I mean . . . like if you're not white and 21, you know, forget it.

And this is what they do. This is what they do. They turn you into a fighting machine and it's, it's so, it's so hideous, some of the things. I mean we've gone into barracks and we've had like pictures of—well, they weren't pictures, they were like cartoons, with slant eyes, you know. Everything was a slant-eye and these little hats on the top, you know. And these were the people you were hating. They were positioned right above the gun racks, you know. No uniform or anything, just, just simply the profile of one, or maybe the face, full face of another. And this, this went on, you know for 16 straight weeks. By the time I had left Ft. Polk, Louisiana, I wanted to kill my mother, you know. Or anyone, that, that wasn't, you know, completely in agreement

157

with me. I wanted to just kill everything, you know. It's really bad.

I went over to Vietnam with the same attitude because I, I had been trained and I knew I was an effective fighting machine. That I was going to kill everything in my path and it started out and it, it lasted for about one day. When I got there and saw the shit being beat out of a few children, you know. And from there on, it was all downhill and, man, like I was a great American, and I think I still am a great American, you know. Just because you don't completely agree with something you don't understand, there was no reason why, you know, you should be a Communist and write with your left hand.

And it's really wild. Through Vietnam these things just kept going and going on and going on. I can relate to you shit that went on. I mean, like, you've gone through this, right? You've gone through the whole thing. But even the people that were on our side, man, even the people that were fighting with us, were still lower class, second-class citizens, you know. Since there weren't that many, they were a complete different race. We would call them niggers, you know, in this country. Over there we call them gooks, you know. It's the same thing. They're second-class citizens. It's a complete racism thing, you know.

Okay, so what happened? Like even the people that are supposed to be on our side, they're supposed to be fighting with us. Right? I have an example here. This isn't an atrocity. You know, it isn't blood and gore. We went into a village and we searched, we searched the people, and not everyone understandably could be in the military because someone had to, you know, work the land. Someone had to provide the food. Okay, who was going to do this? It was people—it was people that, you know, had special permits, special passes, special ID cards. Now these are the people that are on our side. We went into a village and we took the ID cards off of people and sent them back to the rear. I have one here that the press can verify after. I'd like to know what happened to this man. Not this man, but all of our yellow brothers. It's just a big racism thing. You know, they're all complete

158

second-class citizens and it's really, really hideous, you know. There's a number of things.

And then, when I come out of the service, and I come back . . . I would go into, you know, the bars, to where my friends used to loaf and, you know, I would hear these same things going on, that went on before I left. But now, things had changed for me, see. Because I had seen what was going on. I had first-hand, you know, witnessed these things, and I wasn't getting it from the Pittsburgh Press or the Pittsburgh Post Gazette or anything like that, man. I had seen it. And my father, my parents, had sent me clippings of these massive massacres that we had committed—my unit, the 198th—which weren't true; you know, simply weren't true. And, the same thing that's been brought up about the body count. Everything is a bunch of lies.

And you get people sitting back here, you know, back here, and, and they believe this stuff and that's why we've got to get out. I really believe it. Like I've said before, you know, I think this is being a true American. I think it's, you know, sticking up for your country. Damn it, I love this country, and I can't see it being run by fascist pigs, you know.

SP/4 Steve Pitkin, 9th Infantry Division

I'm 20, from Baltimore. I served with the 9th Division from May of '69 until I was air-ovaced in July of '69.

I've sort of got a little hassle by the idea of coming up here, sitting down, and telling basically war stories to everybody, because I'm sure, besides the FBI agents that we have in here, most of you people are against the war. Most of you people know atrocities have been committed. The thing I sort of wanted to impress was that there are different sorts of atrocities being committed. It doesn't necessarily have to be in Vietnam, although those are the ones that get the most attention.

Well, what I'm trying to say is one of the saddest experiences I had is when I returned from Southeast Asia and I

159

was waiting to catch a plane from Frisco Airport to Baltimore. It's like two o'clock in the morning or something and four long-haired people came in. And, you know, it's okay with me, but they laughed at me, and in a sense I really had to fight back tears. I didn't say anything. I tried not to let it faze me that much. But we're not tin soldiers, we're people. The people they sent over to Vietnam are blacks; they sent a lot of college graduates and college students over there. I don't know if this is a form of genocide, but believe me, if you look up the definition, it sort of hints to it.

I feel that if people knew more the human part of the American soldier in Vietnam and about the enormous underground and how well organized it is over there, they might have some second thoughts before they called me a pig or before they called me a tin soldier, laughed at me. I figured before I went over to Nam I had a choice of either going to jail or to Canada, or making it over there. I figured that I was doing more in a capacity to attack it over there, in Vietnam, where the problem was actually happening, than I would be sitting in jail. Although, believe me, anybody who does go to jail or does go to Canada has my full support.

I think it's an atrocity on the part of the United States Army (I don't know about the Marines, Navy, or anything else) to allow eight weeks of basic training, nine weeks of advanced infantry training, and then to send you against an enemy that's been fighting in his own backyard for 25 years. The training that they gave us, the infantry, really amounted to nothing but familiarization with the small-arms weapons and the explosives you would use once you got over there. We attacked a mock Vietnamese village in the snow at Fort Dix.

An interesting point: a lot of times when we were put on line to attack a point or something, you were told not to fire until your left foot hit the ground. I remember asking a drill sergeant, "Do they really do this in Nam?" "Yeah, you know." When I got to Nam, it was like black had turned into white because I was totally unprepared. I was put into a recon unit operating in the Mekong Delta. I hadn't been taught anything about the weather, the terrain. I had been

160

taught a little bit about booby traps, but that's really up to the guy who lays them; they can just be anything. It was just a hit and miss thing. You go over there with that limited amount of training and knowledge of the culture you're up against and you're scared. You're so scared that you'll shoot anything, that you'll look at your enemy, and these people that you're sort of a visitor to—you'll look at them as animals. And at the same time you're just turning yourself into an animal, too.

I'd say that's got my head spinning a little right now. The fact that I was actually at one time an animal and that now I have to come back and be civil again and people sort of expect a purpose, and expect you just to have a definite purpose. You know, you're going to school, yeah, you're going to work, yeah. But there's like more and more veterans now that are just finding that there's no purpose, because nobody's ever given us one. The only purpose I had was surviving and getting the hell out.

Pfc. Charles Stephens, 101st Airborne Division

When I came back to the United States in 1967, I knew that some of the things I did in Vietnam I wouldn't have done prior to going over there. At least I don't think I would have done it. But I knew something was wrong because I could still do those things now that I was back here. I had 30 minutes of debriefing, a steak dinner, and a guy patted me on the back and said, "Well, you did a good job in Vietnam. Now you're back home, forget it." It just didn't work that way, because when I was on leave I would get uptight; I'd get very irritable. If someone says something to me, I get real excited sometimes and I can't answer a person. Maybe we'll get into an argument or something, and I can't give them the answer that they want. They start to, you know, like, really pressure me for an answer. I'll get uptight, and I might swing at them. I won't think twice about it 'cause I was taught it's better to give than to receive. A chaplain told me that—"Do unto others before they do unto you."

161

I don't know, 'cause, like I came back here, I went to a psychiatrist. Where was the first one? Well, before I went over, I went to a psychiatrist at Ft. Campbell, Kentucky, because after my paratroop training I thought it was all over. When I got to my unit I was still a cherry, so they threw me out of the window twice with a poncho and told me to make my cherry blast. I went to a psychiatrist the next day because a sergeant reported that he saw me jump out of a window twice.

Well, when I came back from Vietnam, I went to a psychiatrist again because of the things I did, cutting off ears, castration. I was a medic, but we did all this. They wanted to get an accurate body count so you cut the right ear off everyone you had killed. Now, I was taught in Ft. Sam Houston that we just supposed to carry our weapons for our personal protection and our patients' protection, and that we were supposed to treat the enemy the same way we would, like, treat an American soldier.

Several times I had to leave like women lying in hammocks dying, one lady suffering from a chest wound. I know the lady died and there were two babies left unconscious. The lieutenant told us to just go sit up on this hill, and the next day when they were burying the dead, they were burying these two babies too. They were alive when we left that village. We had guys up on top of the hill firing down with machine guns at these people, and at that time it didn't, you know, it really bothered me, but I was afraid to speak on it. And before I realized it, I was doing the same thing.

When I came back here, well, now I'm out of the service, I've been going to the VA for treatment since 1968, and every time I go to a doctor, he says, "Well, you'll be all right in a couple of years, six or seven years, you'll be all right, so don't worry about it." So finally I got one psychiatrist that seemed to, like, really be interested, like in treating the guys. But this guy he's so busy that you can never see him, and then if you go down—I have a peptic ulcer also, that I got in the Army—if you go downstairs for medical treatment, like for my feet or for my ulcer; if I go downstairs for medication, they say, "Well, you don't need any medication because it's all in your mind. It's all psychogenic," they tell me. And that's the ball game.

Steven Rose, 3rd Marine Division

I'm 26 years old and spent four wasted years in the Navy, from 1963 through 1967. I was a Navy corpsman in Vietnam and I'm presently working now at a psychiatric hospital on Long Island.

I think . . . I call the time I spent in Vietnam "dead time." I call it a time when you just function and do things that, hopefully, you won't do when you come back home. As dead time, I think it's sort of emotionalist—you know, your buddy did it, so you can do it. You don't make a big deal of it.

Lt. Larry Rottmann, 25th Infantry Division

I served as Assistant Information Officer for the 25th Infantry Division, based at Cu Chi, Vietnam, from June 5th, 1967 till March 9th, 1968. My duties were to be officer in charge of the division newspaper, *Tropic Lightning News*, the Lightning Two Five monthly news magazine, and the Lightning Two Five ARVN radio program. I was also in charge of division press releases, including photos; officer in charge of visiting newsmen, including television network crews; and a frequent briefer of the division staff on all civilian news media and information matters.

There is a question in many peoples' minds here. They say, "Well, why do you talk now? Why do you come here and tell us these things that happened two, three, maybe four, five years ago? What is your motivation behind it? You want to get on the boob tube? You're on some kind of an ego trip?" You know, why are you here? I'm here, speaking personally, because I can't *not* be here. I'm here because, like, I have nightmares about things that happened to me and my friends.

163

I'm here because my conscience will not let me forget what I want to forget.

I didn't want to talk about it when I first got back, you know, I didn't want to talk about it at all. I didn't watch Cronkite. I went fishing a lot and changed socks two or three times a day, and slept on beds, and ate cheeseburgers. But after a while, it gets to the point where you have to talk to somebody, and when I tried to talk to somebody, even my parents, they didn't want to hear it. They didn't want to know. And that made me realize that no matter how painful it was for me, I had to tell them. I mean, they had to know. The fact that they didn't want to know, told me they had to know.

So I'm here, not as a member of any political group, not as a member of any lobbying group. I'm just here as myself, you know, saying to other people, to other human beings, something that I just have to say. And if you think it's just clearing my conscience, some kind of therapy, you can think what you want. But I got to say it.

VII. CLOSING STATEMENT

M/Sgt. Don Duncan, 5th Special Forces

As most of you know, the purpose of this investigation was to bring some sort of reality as to what the war in Vietnam really means to people that must fight it, to the people that must suffer in it, to the Vietnamese, to the Americans, to all the mothers, fathers, sisters, wives, brothers. To let them know, in fact, what people do in Vietnam, and what it is doing to their sons, as well as to the Vietnamese.

It's tremendously important that this testimony be brought out, and that it be as widely disseminated as possible, to remove once and for all the blinders and the blinds from in front of America's eyes. No president could have sent us, soldiers and others, to Vietnam, had there not been some sort of cooperation or concurrence, passive or active, on the part of a large segment of this country. How that consent was come by is rather irrelevant. The fact is they had it. Whether it was because we were bent by the media, bent by propaganda, or whatever, the point is now the blinders must be removed.

This meeting has been tremendously important. If it ended here today, it would be important. I hope it doesn't, because there is still a lot of important work to be done, namely, to get this information out to the rest of the country. It seems that we're not going to be able to count on the mass media to do that, so it is incumbent on those who were here to do it. It has been important for another reason. We have had an unprecedented number of veterans from the Vietnam war come in contact with each other for the first time. And many of the revelations to which we have been witness have come from these contacts. Men who otherwise never would have stepped forward, knowing that they had company, did step forward. It wasn't an easy thing. I can assure you for most of these people, it was probably as difficult as anything they have ever done in Vietnam—I would say more difficult than anything they ever did in Vietnam.

In the opening statement, you were told that we were going to prove that, in fact, war crimes in Vietnam are not the result of individual, personal aberrations, but are in fact policy of this country. We have presented testimony covering a wide range of war crimes. We have covered a period by actual first-hand testimony from 1963 to 1970—seven years. We find that in 1963 we were displacing population, we were murdering prisoners, we were turning prisoners over to somebody else to be tortured. We were committing murder then, and in 1970 we find nothing has changed. Every law of land warfare has been violated. It has been done systematically, deliberately, and continuously. It has been done with the full knowledge of those who, in fact, make policy for this country. No active step has ever been taken to curtail those acts in Vietnam.

The argument could be made that we have not shown policy, all we have shown is pattern and practice. I think the argument to that is best displayed not by the testimony of the man who holds the rifle on the ground, but think of the bombings; think of the decisions that are behind the man that is carrying that rifle. We built forts in Vietnam to protect villages, or so we told the Vietnamese. And at the first shot fired at Tet in 1968 we destroyed the villages to protect the fort. District Eight in Saigon was leveled, brick by brick, to the ground, to secure an area where Vietnamese, North Vietnamese, and Catholics had come to the South because that was something the Church had told them in 1954. We leveled that area to protect a bridge.

We have listened to some terrible stories here. We have found there are some wondrous ways indeed to inflict pain upon each other. We will call them atrocities, and we will call them war crimes. And to talk about those acts, I'm sure, has been almost as painful for those who have had to listen as for those who have talked about them. I only hope you will do something with that knowledge now.

In Vietnam we have a situation where never has there been such a disparity of power since the days when Mussolini

166

and Count Ciano went in to Abyssinia to slaughter the spear-carrying troops of Haile Selassie. We have brought wondrous tons of ordinance—hundreds of thousands of men—Dr. Strangelove weaponry. We have used an air force against a country that has none. We have used a navy against a country that has none. And it still wasn't enough, and still the war goes on, and still the Vietnamese fight. It has been called a war of attrition. All wars are wars of attrition. A war of attrition in an industrial society means, in fact, destroying the means of waging war—the factories, communication lines, the roadways, bridges, the iron factories, and so on. In a nonindustrial society—in an agrarian society such as Vietnam—when you talk of a war of attrition, you're talking only of one thing. You're talking about destroying the means to resist—that is, killing people.

Our country has set out very systematically to kill whatever number of people are necessary in Vietnam to stop them from resisting whatever it is we are trying to impose on that country. This, I think, is policy. I think we have established that policy here at these hearings; for those of you who have never been in service and have listened to this testimony, you might well be amazed at how our people—our men, our boys, our sons—could do some of these things that they described in this room. Otherwise normal individuals, creating terror, torture, destruction, wanton. How could they have done this? How could they have been changed that dramatically in eight short weeks of basic training? I think the fact that so much can be done to so many men by so few people is the greatest testament to the fact that our colleges, our high schools, our everyday life is nothing but pre-basic training.

We are well prepared. Whatever it was that was in these men, that allowed them to do the things they did, is in all of us. We start taking it in, if by no other process, at least by osmosis, from the day we are born in this country. The men did not become racists when they entered the service. They grew up with it. It was taught to them and it was taught to them in our schools. The idea that the United States has a God-given right to go into any country and take out its raw materials at an advantage to ourselves is not something that they learned in Vietnam. They learned it in our schools. They learned it from their mothers, fathers, their sisters and their brothers, their uncles. They learned it from all of us.

We did a terrible thing to a lot of men in Vietnam and we're still doing it. I don't know who the ultimate victim in Vietnam will be. Will it be those who went from the United States to fight in it, or the Vietnamese that tried to resist? I do know this, having met and talked with many Vietnamese who have gone through worse hardships than anyone in this room, that they, at least, do not seem to have lost their humanity in the process. But I fear that many of us, if we don't shorten up and get the message out, we will have lost our humanity beyond redemption.

If I can give you a specific example of the insanity of this policy, I think it might explain something. In 1967 (and this deals with this business about what was in these men that might have horrified you, and what is in all of us) Dean Rusk went before the Senate of the United States, trying to explain why we were in Vietnam and what we were doing there; and he made the statement that the reason that we were killing Vietnamese and engaged in a war of attrition against the Vietnamese was because Red China was a threat to the security of the world—meaning us. And some 180-odd million Americans sat in front of the TV tubes and nodded their heads. At last we had the reason why we were in Vietnam. We were in Vietnam to kill Vietnamese because China was a threat to us. He also went on to say that he was not going to allow wars of liberation to succeed, anywhere in the Third World. It's an interesting statement—that it could have been accepted by this country. In fact, I heard very few voices raised against that statement. One of the few that heard was, of all people, Curtis LeMay. Curtis LeMay said we should go and bomb China. Everybody said Curtis LeMay was a madman. But who was the madman? He, having accepted that China was the enemy, thought at least it made sense to go and bomb the enemy. Dean Rusk wanted to bomb the Vietnamese. What a shock this must have been for a lot of soldiers who thought about that statement. Having been told they were going to Vietnam to fight for peace and freedom, they were suddenly told they were going to have to keep fighting Vietnamese until the Bolivians and the Peruvians learned their lesson. And Curtis LeMay was mad.

The terrible thing we did to so many men in this country—and ultimately to the Vietnamese because of it—we sent them to fight a war without a reason to fight it. I don't know how many of you have experienced standing up in front of bullets, exposing your flesh to shrapnel, to hand grenades, and so on. It's a hell of a thing to do, to send out somebody and tell them to make their body a target, and never give them a God damn reason to do it. From 1963 through 1965, the war was fought by professionals, which is to say it wasn't fought at all. Things were going to hell in a bucket. And so they started sending over the draftees, the large units, the people who had to enlist in the military for whatever reason. And they threw them in. For them, taking orders wasn't enough. They wanted a reason. They wanted to believe the reasons they were given. And they accepted those reasons. In fact they urged and begged for a reason. And so they accepted the reasons of freedom and democracy.

The reality of Vietnam, I believe, was a little too much. Anybody in Vietnam for three months, especially in a combat zone, who still believes he's fighting for freedom and democracy, should become a professional. The progress was given. Progress seemed to be enough. Large numbers of troops were sent to various areas of Vietnam, and after three days of battle and God knows how many killed, they would be in possession of that ground. And it was called a victory. The operation was called search and destroy. Quite appropriately. A series of these so-called victories—because we were in possession of the ground, albeit we left it the following day— was called progress. And progress for most, or many, was enough.

And then came Tet of 1968. And in one night, the illusion of progress was gone. Tet could not have taken place without the active or passive cooperation of even the friendly Vietnamese. And who was the enemy? The slopes, the dinks, the zips—the Vietnamese. And all Vietnamese were gooks, slants, slopes, dinks, and whatever. And yet they still had to go out and fight. There was nothing left, not even an illusion of progress. The light at the end of the tunnel turned out to be just what that implies—tunnel vision. And then, we had to keep fighting. For what? We were told, "so we won't be slaves." This isn't the road out of slavery—when you go to fight and kill for absolutely no cause, real or imagined. But in the end, the men keep getting killed. And every day the rage builds up, and the hate grows a little harder. And that rage must vent itself. And who do we blame this rage upon? The captain that gave the order to attack? The people that sent them over there so the captain could give them that order? Or the people who are shooting at you? The Vietnamese are shooting at you, and God damn it, you'll kill Vietnamese, and that's what you're in Vietnam for. So that terrible hatred spills out. And the whole thing not only destroys Vietnamese, it destroys the people who are destroying the Vietnamese. And I feel that it is probably destroying us at a greater and faster rate than it is destroying the Vietnamese.

This country needs scapegoats. It needs a Lieutenant Calley. How can we admit its policy? We need niggers in this country. Who else are we going to kick? Chicanos? Our whole system is built on a principle of racism. To believe that you have the right to go into another country and take from that country, at an advantage to you and a disadvantage to them, you first of all have to believe that those people are something less than you are. Otherwise you'd be guilty of something. And, of course, we're not guilty of anything. Because they are lesser people. When we got tired of the Indians, and there weren't too many of them left to exploit, we went and did it to somebody else. The move westward in this country has moved into Asia. And we're doing it to the Vietnamese, what we did to the Indians. It's oversimplified, but I think it's accurate. We are born with it; we live with it. We have heard testimony relating to another terrible thing. We heard testimony relating to electronic battlefields. Now we're going to kill Vietnamese without using people. And so that the only people who die in this war will be Vietnamese.

We're in Vietnam for a very simple reason. We're in Vietnam, as Dean Rusk says, to prevent wars of liberation from

170

happening in the Third World, anywhere. And why do we have to have that? It is not because the United States is against taking over a country by force. We have proved time and time again that we have no objection to anybody of any political hue taking over another country by force. Just so long as the power that comes into power is cooperative with us on trade relations, etc., to supply the sinews of American industry, to supply the people of this country with all the things they never needed.

To eliminate a nation, to engage in a war of attrition against a people, any people, for such ends as this can only be described adequately with one word. And it's a word that I think falls very harshly on American ears, because we relate it to another incident; and the word, of course, is genocide. Any time you engage in the systematic destruction of a people, that is genocide. The London Agreement and Charter describes war crimes (this is the basis for the Nuremberg Tribunal) as crimes against peace; namely, planning, preparation, initiation, or waging of war, a war of aggression or a war in violation of an international treaty; agreements, or assurances, or participation in a common plan or conspiracy for the accomplishment of any of the foregoing. War crimes, namely, are a violation of laws or customs of war. Such violations shall include, but not be limited to, murder, ill treatment, or deportation for slave labor or for any other purpose, of civilian population of or in occupied territory; murder or ill treatment of prisoners of war, or persons on the seas; killing of hostages, plunder of public or private property, wanton destruction of cities, towns, or villages; or devastation not justified by military necessity. And under the definition of the Charter, we tried the leaders of another nation for war crimes at Nuremberg.

We have heard much testimony to all of those things, here. Again, there is much to be done. And we have to get this information out. I don't want anybody here to carry away a feeling of guilt with them. I want them to carry away the realization of what you have done, and I have done, and why we did it. And I want us all to do something with that. It may look like a hopeless struggle.

171

I remember in 1966, February, I testified to many of the things that have been testified to here. I was very lonely. Thank God, I'm not lonely any more. But still it's a terrible way to gain company—to have men do these things. We have to get it out. Our country has given us very definite proof within the last couple of days, while we have been sitting in this room, that our policies in Vietnam have not changed; that nothing is acceptable to the United States except victory. The Vietnamese have made it quite plain, for almost 2000 years now, that they won't accept victory from an outside power. The [U.S.] policy has not changed. We must change the policy for them. We must get out and talk to these people.

But again, this for many of you, is a first step. There are many things that you as veterans, with this experience, can do. You must not forget that, in fact, there are still 3,000,000 men in uniform. A hell of a lot of them still in Vietnam, and a hell of a lot of them to end up in Vietnam, Laos, and Cambodia. Start working with them. Start working with those who have not yet been drafted, and talk to them, and make the reality of the war known to them. And talk to your families. Over 40 percent of all the adult males in this country are veterans. That's something we have to turn around. We have to stop producing veterans.

And for many of you who have spoken out for the first time and become involved in something for the first time—stay with it. For those of you who are veterans and are working and have been working for some time—keep working. And some day you will be ex-veterans, and we'll just be people again.

APPENDIX

Complete List of Participants in the Winter Soldier Investigation

Pfc. Allen Akers
"E" Co., 2nd Bn., 4th Marine Reg.,
3rd Marine Division
May 1965 to March 1966

Sgt. Joe Bangert
VMO-6, PMAG-39, 1st Marine Division,
1st Marine Air Wing
October 1968 to October 1969

Sgt. John Beitzel
4/21, 11th Brigade, Americal Division
January 1969 to January 1970

Lt. Fred Bernath
101st MP Co., 101st Airborne Division
December 1968 to October 1969

Pfc. William Bezanson
4/3, 11th Brigade
1967 to 1968

L/Cpl. David Bishop
"H" Co., 2nd Bn., 5th Marine Regiment,
1st Marine Division

Cpl. Jon Birch
"B" Co., 3rd Shore Party Bn.,
4th Marine Reg., 3rd Marine Division
May 1965 to August 1966

Maj. Jon Bjornson
     Psychiatrist, Flight Surgeon, USASC,
     8th Field Hospital, Nha Trang
          May 1964 to April 1965

SP/5 David Braum
     21 Trans. Co., 119 Avn. Co. Airmobile,
     52 Combat Avn. Bn., 52 Prov. Plt.,
     Delta Bn.
          1963 to 1964

Pvt. Jack Bronaugh
     "E" Btry. 213, 2nd Bn., 27 Marine Reg.,
     H & S Bn., 7th Marine POW Compound,
     1st Bn., 5th Marine Regiment, MAC-11,
     H & MS-11, 1st Marine Air Wing,
     1st Marine Division
          February 1968 to October 1969

Pfc. Larry Brooks
     2nd Bn., 7th Marine Reg., 1st Marine
     Division
          July 1969 to January 1970

Lt. Sam Bunge
     "B" Co., 3/187, 101st Airborne Division
          July 1968 to June 1969

SP/4 Dennis Butts
     HHQ Co., 2/12, 25th Infantry Division,
     and "E" Co., 4/39, 9th Infantry Div.
          September 1966 to September 1967

Sgt. Tim Butz
     12th Tac Recon Squadron, United States
     Air Force
          November 1966 to June 1968

174

Sgt. Kevin Byrne
    42nd Scout Dog, 1st Brigade,
    101st Airborne Division
        November 1968 to November 1969

CWO Dennis Caldwell
    "A" Trp., 3/17 Air Cav., 1st Aviation
    Brigade
        October 1968 to October 1969

Sgt. Scott Camil
    1st Bn., 11th Marine Regiment,
    1st Marine Division
        March 1966 to November 1967

Cpl. Kenneth Campbell
    "A" Btry., 1st Bn., 11th Marine Regiment,
    1st Marine Division., scouted for "B" Co.,
    1st Marine Regiment, 1st Marine Division
        February 1968 to March 1969

Orville Carey
    1st Logistics Command

SP/4 David Chiles
    3/4, 25th Infantry Division
        January 1968 to December 1968

Jim Clark
    Agency for International Development,
    Catholic Relief Service
        1966 and 1968 and 1969

L/Cpl. Robert Clark
    "H & S" Co., and "G" Co., 2nd Bn.,
    9th Marine Regiment, 3rd Marine Division
        May 1969 and May 1970

175

Ken Clote
Lawyer

David Cohen
Naval Coastal, Division 11
November 1966 to November 1967

SP/4 Douglas Craig
"D" Co., 2nd Bn., 8th Brigade,
1st Air Cav. Division
December 1968 to August 1969

SP/4 Larry Craig
Public Information Office,
25th Infantry Division
August 1966 to September 1967

Pfc. Robert S. Craig
2nd Bn., 5th Marine Regiment,
1st Marine Division
August 1966 to December 1967

Lt. William Crandell
"C" Co. 2/3 Inf., 199th Light Infantry
Brigade, Americal Division

Jay Craven
Student, Boston University, went to North
Vietnam with the National Student
Association
December 1970

SP/4 Allan Crouse
3rd Engineers Brigade, 82nd Airborne
Division
January 1969 to December 1969

SP/4 Jan Crumb
18th Aviation Co.
December 1961 to October 1963

Pvt. Michael Damron
     "B" Co., 3rd Tank Bn., 3rd Marine
     Regiment, 3rd Marine Division
          September 1966 to October 1967

Cpl. Kevin Delay
     H & S Co., 3rd Bn., 1st Marine Regiment,
     1st Marine Division
          October 1969 to March 1970

SP/4 Donald Donner
     20th Brigade, 86th Combat Engineers
          August 1967 to July 1968

Lt. Jon Drolshagen
     4/9th Bn., 25th Infantry Division
          1966 to 1967

HM3 Jeff Dubrow
     1st Med. Bn., U.S.S. *Sanctuary*
          June 1969 to June 1970

SP/5 James Duffy
     228 Avn. Bn., 1st Air Cav. Division
          February 1967 to April 1968

M/Sgt. Don Duncan
     5th Special Forces
          1964 to 1965

SP/5 Don Dzagulones
     635th Military Intelligence Detachment,
     attached to 11th Infantry Brigade,
     Americal Division
          January 1969 to December 1969

Sgt. Ted Eckert
     MAG-16, Support Group-17, 1st Marine

177

Air Wing, 1st Marine Division
July 1969 to August 1970

Sgt. Arthur Egendorf
525 Military Intelligence Group, Saigon

Lee Elbinger
Reporter

Mary Emeny
American Friends Service Committee
1967 to 1968

SP/5 Michael Erard
3/503, 173 Airborne Brigade
April 1969 to March 1970

SP/4 Michael Farrell
"A" Co., 2/60, 9th Infantry Division
January 1967 to January 1968

Lt. Jon Floyd
1st Marine Division
July 1964 to December 1969

Lt. Wilber Forrester
11th Marine Regiment, 3rd Marine Division,
Civil Affairs Officer, U.S.M.C.
1968 to 1969

Cpl. David Fortin
H & S 3rd Medical Bn., 3rd Marine
Division

SP/4 Joe Galbally
1/6, 198 L.I.B., Americal Division
October 1967 to April 1968

Maj. David Galicia, MD
    Psychiatrist, 3rd Field Hospital, Saigon
        July 1969 to June 1970

Cpl. John Geymann
    "M" Co., 3/3 Marines, 3rd Marine
    Division
        June to December 1969

Capt. Joseph Grosso, MD
    General Medical Officer, 173rd Airborne
    Brigade, Field Hospital in Nha Trang
        April 1967 to December 1967

SP/5 Nathan Hale
    Americal Division

YN3 Evan Haney
    Naval Support Activity, US Navy,
    Da Nang
        June 1968 to July 1969

SP/4 John Henry
    9th Infantry Division
        September 1967 to September 1969

Sgt. Jamie Henry
    4th Infantry Division

Sgt. Michael Hunter
    "B" Co., 5/7 Air Cav. Regiment,
    1st Air Cav. Division, "H" Co., 75th Rangers
    attached to 1st Infantry Division
        February 1968 to February 1969
        September 1969 to March 1970

Douglas Hostetter
    Vietnam Christian Service, on the

National Student Association Trip to
Hanoi, December 1970
    July 1966 to June 1969

Barry Hopkins
    9th Infantry Division
        January 1969 to January 1970

SP/4 Timon Hagelin
    Graves Registration Platoon, 243 Field
    Service Co., 1st Logistics Command
        August 1968 to August 1969

Sgt. John Hartner
    H & HD 3rd Brigade, H & HD 2nd Brigade,
    4th Infantry Division
        November 1969 to August 1970

Cpl. William Hatton
    Engineer Mn. Plt., FLSG Bravo,
    3rd Marine Division
        October 1968 to September 1969

L/Cpl. Thomas Heidtman
    3rd Bn., 5th Marine Regiment, 1st Marine
    Division
        October 1966 to November 1967

Pfc. Walter Hendrickson
    "F" Co., 2nd Bn., 9th Marine Regiment,
    3rd Marine Division
        November 1968 to April 1969

Arthur Kanegis
    Research Assistant at NARMIC (Nation Action
    and Research on the Complex); a project of
    American Friends Service Organization

Michael Kenny
    2nd Bn., 26th Marine Regiment, 1st Marine
    Division

Lt. John Kerry
    Coastal Sq., Coastal Division, 11 and
    13. U.S.N.R.
        November 1968 to April 1969

SP/4 Gary Keyes
    "E" Troop, 1st Cav. Reg., 11th Brigade,
    Americal Division
        April 1969 to March 1970

SP/4 Eugene Keys
    3/4, 25th Infantry Division
        February 1966 to February 1967

WO Russel Kogut
    155 Assault Helicopter Co.
        May 1968 to March 1969

Pfc. Robert Kruch
    3/21, 196 L.I.B., Americal Division, "A" Co.

Pfc. Charles Leffler
    "G" Co., 2nd Bn, 26 Marine Reg.,
    9th Marine Amphibious Brigade, LRRP attached
    to 1st and 3rd Marine Division
        September 1968 to September 1969

Lt. Mark Lenix
    1/11th Art'y and 2/39 Infantry,
    9th Inf. Division
        1968 to 1969

Dr. Robert J. Lifton
    Professor of Psychiatry, Yale University

Pfc. William Light
  "E" Co., 1/6, 198 L.I.B., Americal
  Division
    May 1968 to June 1969

Sgt. Murphy Lloyd
  "D" Co., 4th Bn., 173 Airborne Brigade
    February 1967 to February 1968

SP/4 John Lytle
  "E" Co., 6/15 Art'y, 1st Inf. Division
    August 1967 to March 1969

Sgt. Robert McConnachie
  2/28th, 1st Infantry Division
    October 1967 to 1968

Sgt. Michael McCusker
  Public Information Office, 1st Marine
  Division
    1966 to 1967

Ronald M. McSheffrey
  9th Infantry Division, 6th Bn.,
  31 Infantry
    1969 to 1970

Sgt. James Mackay
  HHQ 3rd Brigade, 9th Infantry Division
    August 1969 to December 1970

Capt. John Mallory
  1st Sq., 11th Arm. Cav. Reg., 1st Air
  Cav. Division
    May 1969 to May 1970

SP/4 Michael Misiaszek
  1st Brigade, 101st Airborne Division
  (FSSE)
    December 1968 to January 1970

Lt. Scott Moore
2/39th, 9th Infantry Division
1968 to 1969

Sgt. Edmund Murphy
1/6 198 L.I.B., Americal Division
October 1967 to September 1968

Mike Nakayamo
1st Bn., 5th Marines, 1st Marine Division

Dr. Marjorie Nelson
Medical doctor. Worked in Child Day
Care Center, Rehabilitation Center for
Civilians; treated prisoners in Vietnam
captured during the Tet Offense in 1968
October 1967 to October 1969

Pfc. Ron Newton
3rd Brigade, HHQ Co., 704 Maintenance
Bn., 4th Infantry Division
July 1966 to June 1967

L/Cpl. Sean Newton
3rd Bn., 7th Marine Reg., 1st Marine
Division (from February 1966 to December
1966) "D" Co., 1/26, 3rd Combined Action
Group, 3rd Marine Division
August 1967 to August 1968

Sgt. Fred Nienke
"D" Co., 1st Bn., 5th Mor. Reg.,
1st Marine Division (July 1967 to
February 1968); 1st Prov. Rifle Co.,
Mag 36, 1st Marine Division
July 1967 to February 1968

SP/4 Steve Noetzel
5th Special Forces Group Augmentation
May 1963 to May 1964

183

SP/4 Wayne Novick
   1st En., 26th Inf., 1st Inf. Division
      February 1969 to February 1970

Cpl. Paul Olimpieri
   "D" Co., 1st Bn., 5th Marine Regiment,
   1st Marine Division
      1967 to 1968

Pat Ostrenga
   25th Infantry Division

SP/4 Ronald Polosaari
   1/6, 198 L.I.B., Americal Division
      1967 to 1968

Dr. Sidney Peck
   Professor of Sociology, Case Western
   University; Visiting Professor at M.I.T.

Pfc. Bill Perry
   "A" Co., 1/506, 101st Airborne Division
      November 1966 to August 1968

Dr. Bert Pfeiffer
   Professor of Zoology, University of
   Montana; visited Cambodia, Laos, North
   and South Vietnam
      1969 to 1970

SP/4 Steve Pitkin
   "C" Co., 2/239, 9th Infantry Division
      1969 to 1970

Sgt. Ronald Podlaski
   5th Special Forces Group
      April 1968 to April 1969

184

SP/4 Alex Primm
Public Information Office, 1st Logistics
Command, Headquarters
September 1968 to June 1969

SP/4 Donald Pugsley
5th Special Forces
October 1969 to December 1968

SP/4 William Rice
3/47th, and HQ, 3rd Brigade, 9th Infantry
Division
January 1969 to January 1970

SP/4 Carl Rippberger
K Troop, 3rd Squad, 11th Armored Cav. Reg.,
attached to 9th Inf. Division
May 1967 to 1968

Lt. Barry Romo
"A" Co., 2/1, 196 L.I.B., "C" Co., 3/4,
11th Inf. Bde., Americal Division
July 1967 to 1968

Earl Rose
3rd Marine Division

Steve Rose
E-5 (U.S.N. Corpsmen) HQ Bn.,
4th Marine Reg., 3rd Marine Division
December 1966 to December 1967

Lt. Larry Rottmann
25 Infantry Division

SP/4 Kenneth Ruth
1st Air Cavalry Division
September 1965 to September 1967

Capt. Ernie Sachs
    Medium Helicopter Squadron 362, Marine
    Air Group 36, 1st Marine Division
        August 1966 to September 1967

SP/4 Samuel Schorr
    86th Combat Engineers, 20th Brigade
        September 1966 to September 1967

S/Sgt. Franklin Shepard
    5/60, 9th Infantry Division
        March 1968 to August 1969

SP/4 Vernon Shibla
    Public Information Office, 25th Infantry
    Division
        1966 to 1967

L/Cpl. Scott Shimabukuro
    "C" Btry., 1st Bn., 13th Marine Regiment,
    3rd Marine Division
        October 1967 to November 1968

Cpl. Christopher Simpson
    "E" Co., 2nd Bn., 5th Marine Regiment,
    1st Marine Division
        1967 to 1968

S/Sgt. George Smith
    5th Special Forces (taken prisoner by the
    NLF in 1963 and released in November 1965)

S/Sgt. Jack R. Smith
    HQ Battery, 12th Marine Regiment,
    3rd Marine Division
        January 1969 to December 1969

L/Cpl Christopher Soares
    "G" Co., 2nd Bn., 9th Marine Regiment,

3rd Marine Division
February 1969 to April 1969

J. W. Spellman
Professor of Asian Studies, University
of Windsor, Ontario, Canada

Sgt. Gary Steiger
366th United States Air Force Dispensary,
Da Nang
June 1968 to 1969

SP/5 David Stark
523 Military Intelligence Detachment
October 1967 to October 1968

Pfc. Charles Stephens
1/327, 101 Airborne Division
December 1965 to February 1967

Sgt. Gordon Stewart
"H" Co., 2nd Bn., 9th Marine Regiment,
3rd Marine Division
September 1968 to August 1969

SP/4 James Umenhofer
2/501, 101st Airborne Division
November 1969 to October 1970

Jon VanDyke
Attorney. Worked in State Department in
1966 on POW matters. Now Visiting Fellow
at the Center for the Study of Democratic
Institutions in Santa Barbara, California

Richard Ward
Foreign Editor, The Guardian; in Vietnam
summer of 1965; in North Vietnam and
Laos, summer of 1970

Virginia Warner
    Mother of James Warner, American prisoner
    of war in North Vietnam

Sgt. Jim Weber
    "A" Co., 1/6 and 1/46, 198 L.I.B.,
    Americal Division
        November 1967 to November 1968

SP/4 Robert Wiktorski
    "C" Co., 2/12 Air Cav. Regiment,
    1st Air Cav. Division
        May 1968 to May 1969

Donald Williams
    United States Army; refused to go to
    Vietnam; went to Sweden

L/Cpl. Paul Williams
    "A" Btry., 1st Bn., 12th Marine Regiment,
    3rd Marine Division
        May 1966 to May 1967

SP/4 Curtis Wingrodski
    59th Scout Dog, 11th Brigade, Americal Div.
        March 1969 to October 1969

SP/4 Doug Wright
    1/6 198 L.I.B., Americal Division

Howard Zinn
    Professor of Political Science, Boston
    University